TRAINING
ENGLISCH

Paul Jenkinson

Textproduktion
9./10. Klasse

STARK

Bildnachweis
S. 8, 11, 13, 29, 32, 39, 60, 62, 72, 73, 75: Paul Jenkinson, Coburg
S. 44: The Book of the Millennium, Vol. 4: 1901–2000. © Helicon Publishing
S. 45: oben: The Book of the Millennium, Vol. 4: 1901–2000. © Helicon Publishing; unten: Foreign + Commonwealth Office/HMSO publication
S. 47: © Bill Caldwell
S. 48: © Patrick Blower/Universal Syndication
S. 50: © The Lowry Collection, Salford
S. 54: oben: The New Statesman, April 16, 2001; unten: Daily Mail, August 2, 2002

ISBN: 3-89449-672-X

Inhalt

Autor: Paul Jenkinson

Vorwort

Liebe Schülerin, lieber Schüler,

du hast im Englischunterricht bereits die gesamte englische Grammatik in ihren Grundzügen kennen gelernt und erweiterst fast jeden Tag dein Vokabular. Was bleibt noch zu lernen? Tatsächlich vieles, denn es sind zahlreiche Fähigkeiten erforderlich, um eine Sprache wirkungsvoll einsetzen zu können.

Mithilfe dieses Buches kannst du an der Verbesserung deiner Textproduktion arbeiten. Jedes Kapitel behandelt ein Thema. Die verschiedenen Aufgabenstellungen werden dir immer wieder im Unterricht und in den Klassenarbeiten oder Schulaufgaben begegnen.

- Wie schreibt man einen guten englischen Aufsatz?
- Wie analysiert man ein Foto oder eine Karikatur?
- Was genau ist ein *Summary* und wie schreibt man es?

Dieses Buch vermittelt dir jetzt eine sichere **Grundlage** dafür, wie man gutes Englisch schreibt. Später kann es sehr nützlich sein, wenn du einen bestimmten Aspekt noch einmal nachlesen möchtest. Es ist also jetzt ein Übungsbuch und später ein Nachschlagewerk.

- Die einzelnen Kapitel geben dir **klare Regeln** und **wertvolle Tipps**, sodass du deinen Schreibstil verbessern kannst.
- Die Übungen behandeln **interessante, abwechslungsreiche Themen**.
- Das Buch enthält **Originalmaterial** aus englischen Zeitungen – Texte, Schaubilder, Karikaturen und Fotos.
- In den Lösungen am Ende des Buches findest du **Musterantworten**, die du mit deinen eigenen vergleichen kannst.

Viel Spaß wünscht dir

Paul Jenkinson

Zusammenfassung • *Summary*

Ein *Summary* ist die Kurzfassung eines Textes. Seine Länge beträgt in etwa 25 bis 30 Prozent der Länge des Ausgangstextes. Das *Summary* eines Textes von 500 Wörtern umfasst also 125 bis 150 Wörter. Das bedeutet, dass nur die wichtigsten Inhalte des Ausgangstextes im *Summary* wiedergegeben werden. Das *Summary* muss aber doch so aussagekräftig sein, dass es einer Person, die den Ausgangstext nicht kennt, eine klare Vorstellung des Textinhalts vermittelt.

Wie fasst man zusammen?

- Folge dem Gedankengang des Textes.
- Begnüge dich mit den Fakten, füge keine eigenen Gedanken oder Interpretationen hinzu.
- Vermeide Wiederholungen, auch wenn sie im Text vorkommen sollten.
- Wandle direkte Rede in indirekte Rede um.
- *I* wird zu *he/she* (3. Person).
- Verwende das Präsens, um Texte zusammenzufassen.
- Verkürze jeden Abschnitt auf 25 bis 30 Prozent.
- Verwende deine eigenen Worte, soweit dies möglich ist.

Tipps

- Lies den Text zunächst mehrmals, um ihn vollständig zu verstehen.
- Unterstreiche die wichtigsten Punkte.
- Schlage unbekannte Wörter nach.
- Versuche, den Text durch kurze Ausdrücke zu kürzen.
- Arbeite den Text Absatz für Absatz durch.
- Wenn die Länge des *Summary* in der Aufgabenstellung vorgegeben ist, dann halte dich unbedingt an diese Wortzahl.
- Lies dein *Summary* und frage dich: Ist es kurz und prägnant? Kann jemand, der den Text nicht gelesen hat, anhand meines *Summary* das Wesentliche verstehen? Habe ich den Text in meinen eigenen Worten wiedergegeben?

Exercise 1 Replace the underlined parts of the sentences with a suitable word from the list.
empty, excellent, tired, drove, terrible, noises

a) The woman got into her car and went to the supermarket.

____

b) The weather was grey, wet and windy. The rain poured down outside.

____

c) He looked as if he had slept badly and could not stay awake.

____

d) The CD was the best yet. It was lively with interesting songs.

____

e) Although the house had no furniture in it and no one had lived there for a long time, inside it there were still many sounds – animals moving about and broken windows rattling.

____

____

Exercise 2 Summarise the following short texts. Remember that *I* is replaced by the 3rd person.

a) *(a woman)* I didn't really like the film very much. I thought it missed out a lot of the details and the actors were not like the characters in the story. The book was much better.

b) She laughed, "Last time I saw him, he was in France looking, well, sort of French. Pseudo-French actually – striped T-shirt, beret, baggy trousers, no socks. I thought 'what a mess'. I still think 'what a mess' but, then again, he's happy living there, so I shouldn't really laugh at him, should I? At least he found what he wanted."

c) *(a man)* After walking for hours, wet, cold and miserable, I was glad to see the welcoming light shining out of the windows of the isolated farm. As I got nearer I could smell the wood smoke from the fire inside. Already I felt warmer, the cold had almost left me. As I reached the old, broken down door of the farm the cold returned, but is wasn't an ordinary cold. This was the cold of fear.

Exercise 3 Read the text carefully.

Maximillian Forsyth-Brown. How he hated that name. He'd endured it all his life so far: all sixteen years of it. How could anyone seriously say the name Maximillian Forsyth-Brown without raising their head slightly, putting their nose in the air and spluttering out the words like a dying carp struggling for air?

Just then the doorbell rang. "Hi, is Max in?"

"I'll just get him for you, James," said Mrs Forsyth-Brown as she looked disapprovingly at the young boy dirtying her front doorstep before turning around to call Max.

"Maximillian, it's James for you."

How he hated that tone his mother put on. Why couldn't she be like everyone else and just say Max? Max! Not Maximillian, who sounded like a little soft kid from the posh end of town – and why couldn't she ever use his friends' proper names: Jim, Pete, Jas, not James, Peter and Jaswander?

a) Vocabulary: connect the following words and expressions with their meanings.

1 (to) endure	A upper-class area
2 (to) frown at	B something that one has had to live with that one does not like at all
3 (to) put on	C (here) gentle, almost weak / not tough
4 (to) splutter	D speak with difficulty
5 posh end	E to show your dislike by the face you make
6 soft	F (here) used / adopted

1	2	3	4	5	6

b) Summarise the text in about 60 words.

Exercise 4 a) Read the newspaper text carefully. Mark the points you feel are important.

Age of the five-TV family as teenagers create hi-tech dens

Once, families gathered around their television set and, as it slowly warmed up, discussed – or more often argued about – what they should watch. But those quarrels have gone the way of black and white sets. For the average British family with children over 16 now has five televisions in the house, researchers have revealed. And it is commonplace for older teenagers to have their own – along with an array of other hi-tech gadgets – in their bedroom, which they regard as their private domain.

Experts say children see television as an essential part of life, and because sets are now relatively cheap, they are increasingly being watched in lounges, bedrooms and kitchens.

'Television is like a utility to children, just like electricity is to adults,' said child psychologist Dr Brian Young. 'They are used to it in every room.'

Richard Perkes, of retail analysts Mintel, said that as more and more families invest in flatscreen sets, their old models become available for their children to have in their bedrooms. 'It's partly that they're cheap, partly the growing need to have one in every room, and the change in technology,' he added.

Another factor is central heating. Once an expensive luxury, it is now enjoyed by millions – meaning bedrooms are no longer like iceboxes and the living room is not the only place to watch television on chilly evenings.

But teenagers do enjoy communal viewing – with their friends. The researchers describe the modern teenager as highly territorial, with the bedroom serving as a 'hi-tech lounge' which is strictly off-limits to parents. Designed for socialising with friends, these rooms are full of electronic gadgets and games.

More than half (52 per cent) of the children surveyed had a television, hi-fi system, video or DVD player, games console, personal computer plus a sofa bed installed to impress their regular guests.

The countrywide survey focused on families with teenagers aged 16 and over still living at home.

322 words

b) Vocabulary: what do the following words from the text mean?

den: ______________________

quarrel: ______________________

array: ______________________

gadgets: ______________________

essential: ______________________

communal: ______________________

territorial: ______________________

off-limits: ______________________

(If there are any other unknown words, look in a dictionary to find out what they mean.)

c) Summarise the text to about one-third of the original length.

Dialoge, Monologe und Gespräche • *Monologue, Dialogue and Conversation*

Die direkte Rede umfasst Monologe, Dialoge und Gespräche. Was sind die Unterschiede?

- Monolog *(monologue):* eine lange Rede, die von einer Person gehalten wird
- Dialog *(dialogue):* Gespräche zwischen zwei oder mehr Personen, geschrieben oder gesprochen, als Teil eines Buches oder Theaterstückes
- Gespräch *(conversation):* informelle Unterhaltung zwischen zwei oder mehr Personen

Anführungsstriche *(inverted commas)*

- Die Rede einer Person wird in Anführungsstriche gesetzt. Du kannst einfache oder doppelte Anführungsstriche verwenden, bleibe dann aber bei der einmal gewählten Art. Anders als im Deutschen setzt du im Englischen die Anführungsstriche auch am Anfang der wörtlichen Rede oben.

  Beispiele: 'Hi, how are you?'
  "Hello, it's a nice day today, isn't it?"

- Anführungsstriche sind immer das Erste und das Letzte, was du schreibst, wenn du direkte Rede verwendest. Jedes andere Satzzeichen steht innerhalb der Anführungsstriche.

  Beispiel: "What have you done?"

- Wenn du innerhalb der wörtlichen Rede jemanden zitieren möchtest, hast du, was die Anführungsstriche betrifft, zwei Möglichkeiten:

  Beispiele: 'My mother always said, "Jilly, don't do that" but I never listened to her.'
  "My mother always said, 'Jilly, don't do that' but I never listened to her."

- Verben, die die wörtliche Rede als solche kennzeichnen, z. B. *she said,* werden durch Komma oder andere Satzzeichen, z. B. Fragezeichen oder Ausrufezeichen, von der direkten Rede abgetrennt.

  Beispiele: She said, "I need someone to help me."
  "Can I help you?" he replied.
  "Maybe," she answered.

Groß- und Kleinschreibung

Die wörtliche Rede beginnt immer mit einem Großbuchstaben. Wenn ein die wörtliche Rede kennzeichnendes Verb innerhalb der direkten Rede steht, geht der Satz danach aber mit einem Kleinbuchstaben weiter.

Beispiele: She said, "When do you go to the cinema?"
"You can see," she said, "everything is now OK."

Gedankenstrich und Ausrufezeichen (*dash and exclamation marks*)

- In gewissen Situationen kann ein Gedankenstrich in der wörtlichen Rede etwas hervorheben. Er verbindet eine Aussage mit einer zweiten. Zu viele Gedankenstriche gelten allerdings als stilistisch schlecht.

  Beispiel: "Get me my camera – please."
  "Get me my camera, please."

- Ausrufezeichen werden bei starken Emotionen und Ausrufen verwendet und betonen das Gesagte. Sie werden im Englischen allerdings seltener verwendet als im Deutschen.

  Beispiel: "Run away quickly. Quickly, I said!"

Absätze (*paragraphs*)

Mit jedem Sprecher beginnt eine neuer Absatz.

Beispiel: Peter said, "What a lovely day." Then he went on talking to his wife.
The stranger then spoke again, "Can you help me?"

Exercise 1 Put the correct punctuation into the following sentences:

a) Jenny said run as fast as you can
b) It was an impossible job Mike replied
c) Where have you been asked Lucy quietly
d) My book Kevin shouted is on my desk
e) Mary screamed run now
f) You want me to do that now when I've got no time Mark said angrily

Exercise 2 Punctuate the two dialogues and write them in the correct style. A slash (/) shows where sentences end.

a) what can we do today asked Kim / good question replied Tom / what shall we do / we could go to the cinema but I've seen all the films that are on Kim said / Tom looked in the newspaper and then said what about a football match Manchester are playing against some German team

b) the rain and the wind were terrible / Linda and John had not expected the weather to be so bad / they had left the harbour only half an hour ago in sunshine / oh John when is it going to stop cried Linda it's horrible really horrible / look Linda we can either try to get back to the harbour or sail to that little island, over there John replied / but whatever we do we've got to get out of this storm / John I'm scared / what if we sink / John spoke softly to Linda it's not that bad yet Linda but we've got to get to safety before it gets any worse

Das Entwerfen eines Charakters (*character building*)

Wenn du eine Person entwirfst, musst du Folgendes beachten:

- Alter: Wie beeinflusst das Alter Einstellungen, Meinungen und Redeweise?
- Hintergrund: z. B. reich oder arm, gebildet oder ungebildet. Welche gesellschaftliche Stellung hat die Person?
- Persönlichkeit und Verhalten: z. B. aggressiv oder freundlich, extrovertiert oder introvertiert
- äußere Erscheinung: z. B. schmutzig oder sauber

Exercise 3 Write eight words that could describe a person's appearance, background, personality and behaviour.

appearance	background	personality and behaviour
dirty	*rich*	*aggressive*

Exercise 4 Imagine three characters: a tramp, a shop assistant and a famous pop singer. Make a character study of each person using the criteria of age, appearance, background, personality and behaviour.

character	age	appearance	background	personality and behaviour
tramp				
shop assistant				
pop singer				

Exercise 5 Look carefully at the illustration.

a) Make a character study of the person using the criteria that you know.

b) Write five words or phrases that you could use to describe the person's thoughts or feelings in the illustration? Describe each word or phrase further by using an adverb or an adjective.

thoughts or feelings	described further
hurt	*badly hurt*

Einen Dialog überzeugend schreiben

Wenn du wörtliche Rede schreibst, sprich dir die Sätze vor.

- Klingen sie so, wie sie jemand wirklich sagen würde?
- Passen sie zu der jeweiligen Person?
- Treffen sie den richtigen Ton?

Wenn das, was du geschrieben hast, nicht überzeugend klingt, solltest du

- Kurzformen statt Langformen verwenden (z. B. *don't, can't*),
- Sätze kürzen, sodass sie realistischer klingen,
- wichtige Wörter und Ausdrücke stärker betonen,
- den Wortschatz deiner Person verbessern oder vereinfachen.

Exercise 6 Imagine you know the man in the illustration from exercise 5 and you have entered the room where he is sitting. Continue the dialogue for at least 150 words.

"Hello, Jack. Is everything OK? You look a bit sad."
"Just thinking."
"Thinking about what? You look really sad. What's wrong?"
...

Einen Dialog innerhalb eines Textes schreiben

Wenn du einen Dialog innerhalb eines Textes schreibst:

- Verwende nicht immer *he/she said*. Einige einfache Alternativen sind: *replied, answered, shouted, called out* und *whispered*.
- Füge Adverbien zu *said* und den Alternativen hinzu, um Szenen und Charaktere zu entwickeln.

  Beispiele: She said quietly. He replied nervously. They looked shocked before answering.
- Füge Einzelheiten in das Gespräch und den Text ein.
- Denke daran, dass mit jedem Sprecher ein neuer Absatz beginnt.

Exercise 7 Look at the dialogue that you wrote for exercise 6. This time tell the story as if you were remembering it. Make the story more interesting by adding details using adverbs and replacing "said" with alternatives.

As I entered the café I saw the old man sitting by himself. "Hello, Jack. Is everything OK?" I asked. It was clear everything wasn't OK but I still continued speaking. "You look a bit sad."
"Just thinking," was the answer he gave, without even looking at me.
"Thinking about what?" I replied, but then I saw his face. "You look really sad. What's wrong?"

...

Um einen guten Monolog oder Dialog oder ein gutes Gespräch entwickeln zu können, musst du die Situation bedenken, in der sich deine Charaktere befinden. Sind deine Charaktere z. B. fröhlich oder traurig, wirkt die Situation beängstigend? Welche Atmosphäre möchtest du schaffen, z. B. eine mit Spannung geladene, eine alltägliche, eine düstere?

Darstellung von Situationen

- Verwende Adjektive und Adverbien, um Szenen darzustellen.

  Beispiel: She walked to the house and knocked on the door.

  She walked quickly to the old and broken down house and knocked lightly on the half-opened door.

- Wenn du eine Situation entworfen hast, stelle dir vor, wie dein Charakter in dieser Situation handeln wird.

  Beispiel: (She walked to the house and knocked on the door.) "Hi, is anyone, there?" "Maybe. Who wants to know?"

  (She walked quickly to the old and broken down house and knocked lightly on the half-opened door.) "Hello," she said, whispering as she spoke. "Hello? Is anyone at home? Hello, can anyone hear me? Hello."
  An old, scared voice replied. "Maybe. Maybe there's someone here. Then maybe there's no one. Who are you? What do you want? What are you doing here?"

Exercise 8 Think of two different situations where each of the following sentences could be used. Write down both sentences so that there is a clear difference between them.

a) "What do you want?"
For example: *He stared at the stranger and whispered quietly, "What do you want?"*
She laughed and said, "What do you want?"

b) "I can't talk anymore."

c) "It's dark and there's a funny smell."

d) "Help, someone! Someone help!"

Exercise 9 Imagine that you are in the hot-air balloon with a friend. Your friend is the balloonist but it is your first time in one.
Give five words or phrases to describe your feelings and thoughts and those of your friend's. Think carefully about how they would differ.

	feelings	thoughts
me		
my friend		

Exercise 10 Build three conversations around the hot-air balloon adventure. Try to imagine what you and your friend would say to each other. Think about how you and your friend would feel and react at the following times:

a) You and your friend are talking together and your friend invites you to go ballooning.

b) In the middle of the journey.

c) You are in the basket and suddenly there is no wind. The balloon is quickly losing height getting nearer and nearer the trees.

Wenn du Dialoge schreibst, musst du vieles berücksichtigen. Es geht nicht nur um das Schreiben einer Geschichte, sondern du musst auch überlegen, wie die Charaktere reagieren. Einige Dinge solltest du unbedingt beachten:

- Gibt es irgendwelche Einschränkungen, z. B. eine Begrenzung der Wortzahl?
- Wer sind die Charaktere und welche Eigenschaften haben sie?
- Wie ist die Szene oder die Atmosphäre, die geschaffen werden muss?
- Verfolgt der Dialog ein Ziel? Wie kannst du dieses Ziel erreichen? Wenn du in der Erarbeitung deines Dialogs völlig frei bist, welches Ziel strebst du an?
- Lies dir den fertigen Dialog immer laut vor, um zu kontrollieren, ob er realistisch klingt.

Wenn du am Inhalt arbeitest, solltest du Folgendes beachten:

- Was willst du sagen?
- Wohin führt das Gespräch?
- Was ist der Zweck des Gesprächs?
- Wie kannst du das Gespräch interessant und abwechslungsreich gestalten?

Exercise 11 It is easy and fun to add speech bubbles to photographs. Study the example and then write your own idea.

Exercise 12 What do you think the two boys are talking about?

a) Write their comments in the speech bubbles.

b) Continue the conversation between the two boys as a written dialogue.

Exercise 13 Write a dialogue for the following situation:

On holiday in Scotland you visited the Loch Ness Monster museum. You saw many photographs of Nessie and they gave you the idea of playing a trick on your best friend. You decide to tell your friend that you really saw the monster when you were at the side of the loch. Naturally, you need to build up to this carefully. Consider:

- telling your friend first about the time of day and the atmosphere
- explaining what Loch Ness looks like
- how to get your friend to believe in the monster
- how your friend might react

Exercise 14 Write a ghost story, which includes dialogue, using the given information.

You were travelling with friends in their car when it suddenly stopped. You are the person who tries to find a telephone to phone for help. You find a lonely house. The house has a strange atmosphere. There is an old person inside. The old person always talks about strange things. You leave without using the phone and go back to the car. Your friends are, of course, angry with you for not getting help.

Tagebuch schreiben • *Diary entries*

1 Was ist ein Tagebuch?

Ein Tagebucheintrag enthält die persönlichen Gedanken und Gefühle des Verfassers. Häufig werden darin wichtige Ereignisse im Leben des Verfassers festgehalten. Ein Tagebuch ist nicht immer spontan geschrieben, es kann umgeschrieben und mehrmals neu durchdacht werden, bevor es seine endgültige Fassung erhält.

Stil

- Am Anfang eines jeden Tagebucheintrags steht das Datum.
- Halte dich an einen einmal gewählten Schreibstil (z. B. ernsthafte persönliche Gedanken, humorvolle Annäherung an ein Thema, subjektive oder objektive Aufzeichnung von Ereignissen).

Inhalt

- Falls du die Wahl hast, solltest du über interessante Themen schreiben.
- Stelle ganz gewöhnliche Situationen lustig oder aufregend dar, indem du auf Einzelheiten achtest.
- Drücke deine Gefühle aus und gib deine Gedanken und deine Meinung wieder.
- Falls du ein Tagebuch aus der Sicht einer anderen Person schreiben sollst: Versuche, dich in diese Person hineinzuversetzen, und überlege, wie sie aufgrund ihres Charakters reagieren könnte.

Tipps

- Überlege, warum du ein Tagebuch schreiben sollst – behalte dieses Ziel im Auge.
- Gibt es irgendwelche Beschränkungen für deinen Tagebucheintrag (z. B. eine vorgegebene Wortzahl)?
- Es ist äußerst schwierig, in einer Fremdsprache humorvoll zu sein; häufig ist es daher einfacher, sich auf Tatsachen und eine formellere Schreibweise zu beschränken.

2 Vokabular, Satzbau und Stil

	informeller Eindruck	**formeller, gebildeter, wohldurchdachter Eindruck**
Vokabular	• leichtes Vokabular • Kurzformen	• anspruchsvolleres Vokabular • Synonyme • Langformen
Satzbau	• einfache Grammatik • kurze Sätze	• kompliziertere Grammatik • längere Sätze
Stil	• umgangssprachlich • schreibe, als ob du dich unterhältst	• betrachtet Ereignisse aus der Distanz • Stilmittel: stelle Fragen, bilde kurze Sätze, um Wirkung zu erzielen, verwende Metaphern

Exercise 1 Using the simple sentences provided write two alternative ones using the same theme as if you were making an entry into your diary: one with a formal style, the other with an informal one.

For example: It was a wet day.
It was one of those days when the rain simply did not stop. (formal)
What a horrible day – the weather's terrible. (informal)

a) There is a lot of noise outside.

b) Those two girls are always playing with their mobile phones.

Exercise 2 Extend the information in the sentences below and provide two diary entries of two or three sentences in length for each theme: one formal, the other informal.

For example: The theatre performance at your school was very good.
The theatre performance finished last night at my school. Although it was tiring and involved a lot of work, it was very successful. (formal)
At last the performance is over. I'm really tired but it was fun and everyone liked it. (informal)

a) Yesterday your friend, Jenny, broke her leg walking down the street.

b) Your bike got a puncture and you have had to push it 3 kilometres home.

Exercise 3 Write about 50 words using two different styles on each of the following sentences explaining how you feel about the situation:

a) You must be home by 11 p.m. at the weekends.

b) All young people will have to do one year's voluntary work in the future.

Exercise 4 Write about 100 words more completing the following diary entries. Keep to the different styles. Theme: *A boring day.*

9th February 2004

What a day! It began boring, became more boring and ended up even more boringly. Have you ever thought what you can do when there's nothing to do? The shops are shut, I've read all ...

9th February 2004

What is it that makes a day boring? Is it that there is just nothing to do or is it that one wants something extra: something new to stimulate the mind, something to get excited about? Why do we handle some days so badly? Today is boring. It is not that there is nothing to do, it is just that ...

Exercise 5 Provide a diary entry for each of the following themes. You may write in whichever style you feel comfortable with.

a) the accident

b) being ill on holiday

c) the first snow of the year

3 Tagebucheintragungen aus der Sicht einer anderen Person schreiben

Wenn du aufgefordert bist, aus der Sicht einer anderen Person zu schreiben, beachte Folgendes:

- Welchen Charakter besitzt diese Person?
- Welche Gefühle hätte diese Person?
- Gibt es eine besondere Situation?
- Wie ist der äußere Rahmen (z. B. Jahr, Umgebung, Atmosphäre)?

Beispiel:

Write a diary entry as: Leonardo da Vinci after painting the Mona Lisa.

Character: (Leonardo da Vinci) artistic, different, creative, intense …
Feelings: happiness, pleased, satisfied …
Other aspects: Mona Lisa, who is she? she is now famous, the smile, the date …

23rd March 1506
Finished at last. There were days when I thought I could never capture Mona's smile. I stand back from the canvas now and cannot believe I have painted such a face. I remember starting out on the picture in 1503, summer it was because I had a problem with the light. But although I have done many other paintings between then and now, this is my best. I'm truly stunned at my own work. What I cannot understand is that Mona refuses to have anything more to do with the picture. She doesn't want to be known as the person in it.
A shame, she has such a beautiful smile.

Exercise 6 Write a diary entry as a different person. Make notes about the character and the situation before you begin.

a) a homeless person
b) someone who has just climbed Mount Everest
c) the architect of the leaning tower of Pisa

Exercise 7 Read the interview carefully.

Worth the Wait

(Fame Academy is a school for people who want to become pop singers. The 'students' are taught how to improve their talent. Each week, on television, they must perform and then are criticised and a winner is chosen. Lemar is one of the 'students'.)

Lemar, what is your fondest memory from your time in Fame Academy?
My nicest experience in there was dueting with Lionel Ritchie. That was extremely good, he was a nice guy and gave me some great advice.

You seemed like a rather cool cat on TV, but did you ever get nervous?
Oh, yes, I was nervous. But I'm not one of those people who shouts about it. When they told me I was going to sing with Lionel Ritchie, I was genuinely excited. I was nervous before the performance and in the rehearsal, just before the live show, I forgot all the words. But Lionel spoke to me and helped me calm down. During the actual show, it was more like singing with a friend – I was calm and chilled.

Head teacher Richard Park obviously had his favourites and you weren't one of them – but you lost your temper only once. How did you keep so calm?
It's a funny situation. You spend your whole week trying your hardest, listening to what they have to say and trying to take in all the aspects of what they are telling you. But it's hard for them as well because they support you all week and then, on Friday, they have to turn on you and rip you to shreds. So it was hard, but you had to remember it was a TV show and to hold back your feelings. It's best just to bite your tongue.

Did the feedback that you got from guest stars such as Shania Twain and Mariah Carey help?
Oh, yeah. Shania pulled me to the side during the live show and told me to forget about what was going on and to just keep doing my thing. That was really nice.

Were you surprised you only came third?
No, it happened like I thought it would. I didn't expect to win and I was ready for it. Although, on that final evening, it's the one time I can say that I was nervous. I always thought David would pinch it because he's got that broader general appeal.

When the show finished, did you go back to your normal life?
I didn't go out too much in my area because it was quite hectic. I was also quite nervous because I was waiting for a deal to come. Everyone else got signed really quickly so there seemed to be a big pause. It was scary there for a second and then, finally, a couple of offers came in. 422 words

Annotation: Lionel Ritchie, Shania Twain and Mariah Carey are all successful singers

a) Vocabulary: which explanation goes with the following words or phrases from the text?

1 fondest
2 dueting
3 cool cat
4 calm down
5 chilled
6 rip you to shreds
7 bite your tongue
8 pulled me to the side
9 pinch it

A say nothing
B to criticise you a lot
C best
D relaxed
E took me away from everyone
F relax
G singing with one other person
H just win it
I calm and relaxed person

1	2	3	4	5	6	7	8	9

b) How do you see Lemar's character and the situation? Make notes under the following categories:

Lemar's character: ______________________

his feelings: ______________________

the situation: ______________________

the outcome: ______________________

c) You are Lemar, consider your feelings and thoughts when you write your diary entries for the days and situations mentioned. Make notes for each diary entry before you begin to write.

For example:
Notes for entry 1: *exciting to sing with Lionel Ritchie / he's nice, gives good advice / I was nervous, forgot words, Lionel helped me / tried hard all week / listening/ they support you, but on Fridays they attack you …*

entry 1: about Fame Academy, singing with Lionel Ritchie and up to the live show
entry 2: the performance
entry 3: the result of yesterday
entry 4: some days after the live show
entry 5: many days after the live show and good news

Einen Text mit begrenzter Wortzahl schreiben • *Writing with a limited length*

1 Kurz und bündig schreiben

Wenn du einen Text verfassen sollst, bei dem die Anzahl der Wörter genau vorgegeben ist, solltest du beim Schreiben folgende Punkte beachten:

- Schreibe immer auf das Thema bezogen.
- Überschreite nicht die vorgegebene Wortzahl (etwa 10 Prozent mehr sind akzeptabel, was darüber hinausgeht, ist zu viel).
- Beachte genau die Formulierung der Frage, z. B. *discuss, comment on* oder *express your opinion* (siehe auch S. 25).
- Mache dir Notizen, bevor du anfängst zu schreiben, und gliedere deine Antwort.

Beispielaufgabe:

Write about 150 words on the following topic: Should schools move away from exercise books, pens and pencils and make children use laptops instead?

Worauf zielt die Frage ab?

Es ist gefragt, ob Schüler in der Schule nicht mehr mit Papier und Stift, sondern stattdessen mit Notebooks arbeiten sollten. Die Frage ist allgemein gestellt, daher muss deine Antwort nicht nur deine persönliche Meinung enthalten.

Notizen

Yes: way of the future / important to learn computing / …
No: cost / technology rapidly outdated / …

Gliederung und Aufbau

Auch wenn du nur eine begrenzte Zahl von Wörtern schreiben darfst, sollte dein Text eine (kurze) Einleitung, einen gegliederten Hauptteil und eine Schlussbemerkung enthalten.

- Du musst schnell zu den wichtigen Punkten kommen.
- Ordne deine Argumente oder Ideen logisch.
- Formuliere eine Schlussbemerkung zu dem, was du geschrieben hast, z. B. indem du das Thema noch einmal klar zusammenfasst oder eine deutliche Stellungnahme abgibst.

Eine mögliche Antwort

Computers play an important role in today's society. It is almost impossible to escape using them. Schools should realise that pens and paper will soon be as old-fashioned as chalk and slate.

introduction
short and direct; opinions clearly made without using 'I think …'.

The future is with computers and it is important that children use them from an early age. Having laptops would mean all pupils could do this. Children could correct mistakes easily, always have their work at hand and make good presentations. Ideally pupils should have Internet access, too.

middle section
ordered points; reason for laptops; the advantages; opinions without 'In my opinion …', for example

There are objections which could be made, though. Not all families can afford the high cost, especially where the family is large. Standardisation could be a problem and rapidly changing technology, too. New methods to control pupil's work would be needed and teachers would have to be able to use the technology.

the disadvantages; reasons not to adopt laptops; opinions without 'In my opinion …', for example

Computers will not suddenly disappear, so the time for schools to use them in every lesson is now. *150 words*

conclusion
the conclusion answers the question; the right number of words

Lies und kontrolliere

- Überprüfe deinen Aufsatz auf Fehler. Kannst du ihn noch verbessern?
- Kannst du etwas noch besser ausdrücken?
- Hast du dich an das Thema gehalten?
- Hast du dich an die vorgegebene Wortzahl gehalten? Musst du deine Antwort kürzen oder noch etwas hinzufügen?

Beachte: Es ist nützlich zu wissen, wie viele Wörter du durchschnittlich pro Zeile schreibst, denn dann kannst du während des Schreibens überschlagen, wie lang deine Antwort ungefähr ist.

Exercise 1 How can you make your writing interesting? Think about the topic, "Should town centres be traffic-free?"

a) Which introductions do you think are good, which are acceptable but nothing special and which are poor ones? Compare your opinion with the explanation in the key.

	good	average	poor
I think cars should be banned from town centres because they cause many problems.	☐	☐	☐
Traffic-free town centres are a dream, the reality of achieving them is impossible.	☐	☐	☐
I think, in my opinion, that people with cars should be able to go to the shops in them.	☐	☐	☐
There are too many cars in most town centres and therefore they should be banned.	☐	☐	☐
Without vehicles being able to enter town centres, town centres would stop functioning.	☐	☐	☐
Town centres rely on trade. People bring that trade and vehicles bring people to town centres.	☐	☐	☐
Why should vehicles enter town centres at all? My opinion is that most don't need to.	☐	☐	☐

b) You are given a middle section of an answer to the topic "Should town centres be traffic-free?" which is too long. There are also many filler words, repetitions, points not made concisely and sentences which could be shortened.
Rewrite the text using about 100 words.

Some traffic is necessary in town centres and cannot be stopped. Lorries and vans, for example, must be allowed to deliver things to the various shops and, therefore, they should be allowed to continue. Buses, though, could be limited to one or two special areas near the town centre and, therefore, stay out of the main area. Taxis should also be allowed into the centre. However, all these vehicles should have to travel very slowly in the main areas. Cars, though, cause most of the problems. There should be many alternative car parking areas away from town centres. In larger cities good 'Park and Ride' systems should be available. If people, however, are stopped from driving into town centres, there is a danger that shops there might lose business because many people will then go to shops where they can park nearby: this means large out-of-town shopping centres and supermarkets. These large stores would then see that the banning of cars in town centres is a wonderful opportunity to develop more shops on the outskirts with ample parking. The danger, here, is that people might stop using town centres altogether and many shops will then close. *196 words*

Exercise 2 Write your own answer to the topic "Should schools move away from exercise books, pens and pencils and make children use laptops instead?" using approximately 150 words.

Exercise 3 Write about 160 words on the following topic "What do you see as the main problem facing your country at the moment? How should this be dealt with?".

Before you begin:

- What is the question about?
- Make notes and order them.
- How can you make a good introduction?
- How should you order your points in the middle section?
- How can you make a good conclusion?

When you have finished:

- Read and check your answer.
- Have you written the correct number of words?
- Have you answered the question?

Exercise 4 Write between 150–180 words on the following topic "Do you think that young people today should take every opportunity to go abroad?".

2 Verschiedene Aufsatzarten mit begrenzter Wortzahl

Aufsatzthemen folgen denselben Regeln wie Fragen mit vorgegebener Wortzahl. An folgende Punkte solltest du denken:

- Du musst verstehen, was gefragt wird.
- Weiche nicht vom Thema ab.
- Du musst sinnvoll gliedern und stilistisch gut schreiben.
- Beachte mögliche Einschränkungen, z. B. in Bezug auf die Wortzahl.

Die Formulierung von Aufsatzthemen

Du musst zu vielen verschiedenen Themen Aufsätze schreiben. Bei der Themenstellung werden dir immer wieder Formulierungen wie *express, outline* oder *comment on* begegnen. Lerne, sie zu unterscheiden.

comment on Schreibe über die Situation und diskutiere das Thema. Dabei darfst du aber nicht einseitig argumentieren bzw. Kritik äußern. Bei dieser Aufsatzart ist auch deine persönliche Meinung gefragt.

discuss Schreibe über die verschiedenen Ansichten: Finde vernünftige Argumente für oder gegen das Angesprochene, ziehe eine Schlussfolgerung.

explain Gib Gründe für die Situation an und stelle sie leicht verständlich dar. Bei dieser Aufsatzart musst du klare Informationen geben und auch auf Einzelheiten eingehen.

express your opinion Hier ist nach deiner persönlichen Meinung gefragt, die du aber mit Argumenten stützen musst.

outline Hier musst du einen Überblick über eine bestimmte Sache geben. Verzichte dabei darauf, auf Einzelheiten einzugehen.

summarise siehe S. 1

Exercise 5 Write your opinion and comment on the following topics in one or two sentences.

a) the cost of CDs
For example: *I think CDs are too expensive. If they were cheaper, more people would buy them.* (opinion)
CDs are too expensive. (comment)

b) fashionable clothes in schools

c) all-day schools

d) skiing and the environment

e) Christmas lights and decorations outside shops in November

Exercise 6 Put forward a strong argument for and one against making English the official language of the EU. Do not use “I think …”, “in my opinion …” or any similar phrases in your answer.

Exercise 7 Read the dialogue carefully.

JOHN: When I was in London last week, I read in a newspaper that the latest fashion is long pointed shoes.

LUCY: Yeah. I think they're great. I'd love a pair. They look really cool.

JOHN: Maybe. They're not really my taste, but ...

LUCY: But, what?

JOHN: It's nothing really about the shoes, it's about the people who wear them.

LUCY: Like me, you mean, if I had a pair?

JOHN: No, not like you. About people whose feet don't fit into these shoes because they are so pointed. Some of them even had one of their toes removed. A toe cut off just to fit into a shoe!

LUCY: Amputated! That's horrible. I think you're making the story up.

JOHN: No, I'm not. It was in the paper. I couldn't believe it either.

LUCY: I like fashion – and those shoes – but cutting off a toe to wear them is really stupid. You can't grow a new toe again when pointed shoes go out of fashion, can you?

Using the dialogue as a source of information write a maximum of 80 words on each topic:

a) Comment on the latest fashion trend in Britain.
b) Summarise the latest fashion trend in Britain.
c) Express your opinion on the latest events in Britain.
d) Outline how fashion influences people.

The content of your answers may be similar but you should make sure that what you write answers the question directly.

Exercise 8 Answer the following essay questions. Before you begin study the wording of each question carefully.

a) Young drivers should only be allowed to drive low-powered cars until they have had their licence for three years. Discuss this idea to prevent accidents using about 150 words.
b) Should developed countries stop third-world ones making mistakes which damage the environment? Express your opinion in approximately 200 words.
c) Comment on whether or not there is too much technology used in every day objects. Write between 200–250 words.

Beschreibungen • *Descriptive writing*

Mithilfe von Adjektiven und Adverbien kannst du Situationen, Ereignisse oder Personen treffend beschreiben.

Adjektive

- Sie bestimmen und beschreiben ein Substantiv näher.
  Beispiel: He was an old man.
- Du kannst für eine Beschreibung mehr als ein Adjektiv verwenden.
  Beispiel: He was a scared, old man.

Adverbien

- Adverbien drücken aus, wie etwas getan wird. Sie liefern nähere Informationen über das Verb.
  Beispiel: She walked slowly along the road.
- Du kannst mehr als ein Adverb benutzen, um zu beschreiben, wie etwas getan wird.
  Beispiel: She walked slowly and tiredly along the road.
- Adverbien beschreiben Adjektive näher.
  Beispiel: He is a very bad driver.

Wortschatz

- Finde Wörter, die zur Situation passen.
  Beispiel: Her soft smile warmed people's hearts.
  Her nasty smile made people worried.
- Einige Wörter drücken Verärgerung oder Zorn aus, andere klingen weich und sanft. Versuche zu erkennen, welchen Klang ein Wort hat, z. B. *crashing, banging, softly, smoothly.*

Exercise 1 Improve the following sentences with adverbs. Try not to repeat any that you use.

a) She ran towards the door.
She ran quickly towards the door.

b) The door opened but no one was there.

____

c) They both sat together.

____

d) He was scared but he still entered the building.

____

e) The young woman drove her sports car along the country roads.

____

f) She was happy but sad, too.

____

Exercise 2 a) Develop a word field around the nouns in the list. Write at least four adjectives for each word: *rain, a stranger, a building, a town, a friend, a dream.*

Example:

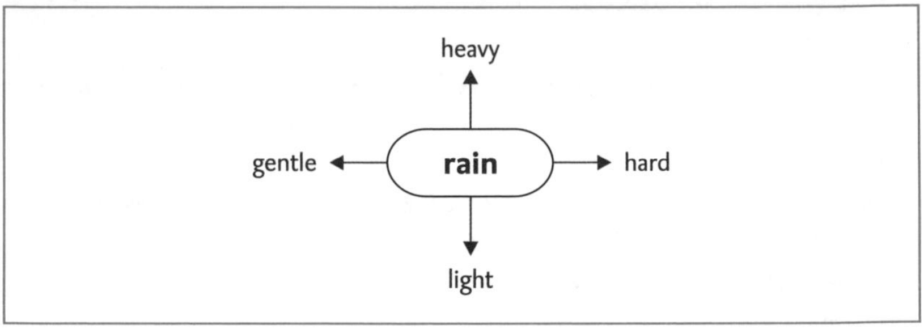

b) Write two sentences for each of the nouns using some of the adjectives you gave in the word field.

Example: **rain: heavy / gentle**

As we drove along the road heavy rain began to fall.
The gentle rain had at last stopped and the sun began to shine.

Exercise 3 a) Look carefully at the photograph of Hogan's Point lighthouse. Describe each of the words given with four different adjectives.

sky: ______ ______ ______ ______

coast: ______ ______ ______ ______

sea: ______ ______ ______ ______

path: ______ ______ ______ ______

lighthouse: ______ ______ ______ ______

b) Describe the photograph in full sentences using some of the descriptive words that you have written in answer a.

sky: It's a calm day at the lighthouse, the sky is cloudy but it remains bright and clear.

c) Write a short descriptive text of approximately 100 words about arriving at Hogan's Point lighthouse for the first time. You may need to add some further information.

For example: *As we arrived at Hogan's Point the weather became calmer. There was still a cloudy sky but it was bright and clear …*

d) Imagine the scene at Hogan's Point in a very bad storm. How would it alter and what descriptive words would you now use? You may need to add more information, for example about the waves. Build word fields for these new words.

For example:

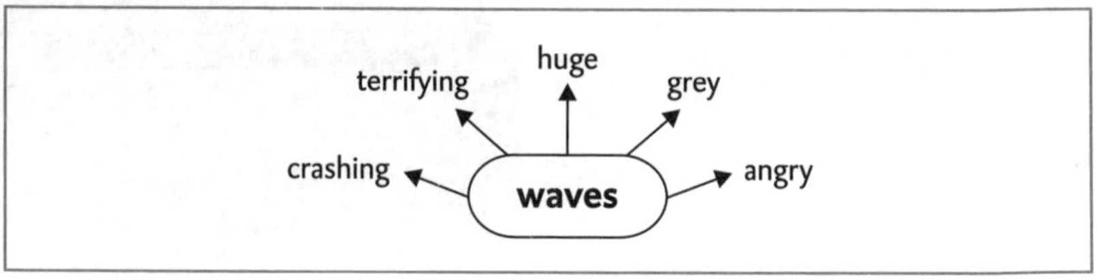

e) Using about 100 words write a new descriptive text about Hogan's Point in a very bad storm.

Exercise 4 Put the most suitable sounding word from the list into the correct sentence: *crashed, silent, banged, fought, screeched.*

a) The car door ______________________ shut.

b) The waves ______________________ down onto the beach.

c) The old woman ______________________ along the busy street to get to the shops.

d) The car's tyres ______________________ as it was driven away in a hurry.

e) There were ______________________ footsteps in the snow.

Exercise 5 Build two sentences around each subject. In the first sentence use two descriptive words and in the second sentence three.

For example:

a) a stranger *His dirty and untidy hair was below his shoulders.*
His dirty, untidy and uncombed hair was below his shoulders.

b) an old man's face ______________________

c) a building ______________________________

____

d) a birthday party ______________________________

____

e) a city centre ______________________________

____

f) the top of a mountain ______________________________

____

Exercise 6 Look around where you are and describe it in detail. Think how you can make even the most boring things interesting.

Example: *pieces of paper on your desk*

Pieces of paper are scattered across my desk like autumn leaves on a pavement. Blown about, then left. They stare up at me, innocently inviting me to tidy them away. But I don't.

Exercise 7 Describe the following simple things and situations as interestingly and creatively as possible.

a) a pencil
Example: *The red pencil lay alone on my desk. It was just another pencil like many others. Ordinary, one could say. One end chewed, the other sharpened.*

b) a book

____

____

c) an old pair of jeans

____

____

d) people meeting at an airport

____

____

e) your mobile phone ringing

____

____

Exercise 8

a) Some situations are difficult to describe and you must think carefully about what you can write about.
The photograph shows the main road on the Isle of Jura, a Scottish island. Study it carefully, build word fields around the given nouns in the list then add any further observations you can make.

	description	**observations**
landscape →	unfriendly	no houses
→		
road		
weather		
telegraph poles		

b) Describe the Isle of Jura in full sentences. Look carefully at the photograph again and the word fields.

c) Either, complete the story or write your own about the road and landscape on the Isle of Jura using about 200 words. Write as descriptively and creatively as you can.

We just couldn't get the wheel off. We'd tried hitting it, kicking it, screaming at it but nothing worked. What a place to get a puncture! Beautiful, but …

Briefe und E-Mails • *Letters and e-mails*

1 Die äußere Form von Briefen

Hier siehst du das Beispiel eines Standardbriefes. Achte dabei besonders auf folgende Punkte:

- Wo stehen im Brief welche Informationen?
- An welchen Stellen wird welche Zeichensetzung gebraucht?
- Wann wird im Brief groß- und wann kleingeschrieben?
- Bei formellen Briefen muss im Briefkopf immer der Adressat enthalten sein. Bei persönlichen Briefen entfällt dies.

24 Castle Street Blackburn Lancashire LK6 5TQ	writer's address
6th March 2004	date
Mrs J. Fox Dane Cleaners 3 Arthur Road Doddington NE3 6LD	recipient's name and address *(formal letters only)*
Dear Mrs Fox,	salutation
Thank you for your letter …	letter
Yours sincerely,	closing
Adam Smith	signature
Adam Smith	name

Die einzelnen Teile des Briefes

- **Absender (*sender's address*):** Die Adresse des Absenders kann mit oder ohne Zeichensetzung geschrieben werden, auf jeden Fall musst du dich für eine Variante entscheiden.
- **Datum (*date*):** Den Monat solltest du ausschreiben. Im amerikanischen Englisch schreibt man zuerst den Monat, dann den Tag und dann das Jahr: March 6th, 2004.
- **Absender und Datum (*sender's address and date*):** Notiere sie am rechten Briefrand untereinander.
- **Empfängername und -adresse (*recipient's name and address*):** Bei formellen Briefen schreibst du den Namen und die Adresse des Empfängers auf den linken Briefrand.
- **Anrede (*salutation*)**
- **Brief (*letter*)**
- **Schluss (*closing*)**
- **Unterschrift (*signature*)**
- **Name (*name*)**

Anrede und Briefschluss

- Wenn du den Namen des Empfängers nicht kennst:
  Verwende für einen männlichen Empfänger '*Sir*', für einen weiblichen Empfänger '*Madam*'. Wenn du dir nicht sicher bist, verwende '*Sir or Madam*'.

Anrede (*salutation*)	Schluss (*closing*)
Dear Sir Dear Madam Dear Sir or Madam	Yours faithfully

- Wenn du den Namen des Empfängers kennst:
  Bei einer verheirateten Frau verwendest du '*Mrs*', bei einer unverheirateten '*Miss*'. Wenn du es nicht weißt, verwendest du '*Ms*'.

Anrede (*salutation*)	Schluss (*closing*)
Dear Mr James Dear Mrs Roberts Dear Miss Berry Dear Ms Bell	Yours sincerely

- Wenn du jemanden gut kennst und ihn mit Vornamen anredest:

Anrede (*salutation*)	Schluss (*closing*)
Dear Jane Dear Mike	Best wishes Love (nur bei sehr guten Freunden und nicht zwischen Männern)

Exercise 1 What is the correct salutation and closing to use for each of these letters? You are writing to:

a) Chris, a friend ______________________________

b) someone at a bank ______________________________

c) a woman named Jones ______________________

d) Mrs Fiona White ______________________

e) a woman in a shop ______________________

f) Mike Petty in a travel agent's ______________________

g) your penfriend (Sue Foster) ______________________

h) a man in an office ______________________

i) Tony Blair's wife ______________________

Exercise 2 Put the information below into a good letter layout.

yesterday, I saw your advertisement in the newspaper for …
6/8/04
John Stuart
dear
sir / madam
yours faithfully
31 Appletree Lane, Norwich, PE67 2ST
(*for*) Computer City, 19 Park Road, Bath, BR2 7FD

2 Aufbau eines Briefes

Briefaufbau

Ein Brief besteht normalerweise aus drei Teilen:

- Mit einem oder zwei Sätzen führst du in das Thema deines Briefes ein. Hier erklärst du, was du möchtest, oder du bedankst dich bei jemandem für seinen Brief, bevor du deinen beginnst.

  Beispiele:
  Thank you for your letter dated (of) 12th August.
  I would like to complain about …
  I am writing an English essay and would like some information about …

  Ein persönlicher Brief an einen Freund wird ganz anders aussehen.

  Beispiel:
  How are you? I haven't heard from you for ages.

- Im Mittelteil gehst du auf die Einzelheiten ein.
  In formellen Briefen verwendest du Langformen, einen gehobeneren Wortschatz, Synonyme, korrekte Grammatik, keine Slangausdrücke, klare und präzise Einzelheiten.
  In persönlichen Briefen werden häufig Kurzformen, einfacherer Wortschatz und einfachere Grammatikkonstruktionen und idiomatische Ausdrücke verwendet. Sie sind persönlicher.

  Beispiele:
  I have been waiting since the end of February for your reply. (formell)
  I haven't heard from you for a long time. (persönlich)

- Der **Schluss** rundet den Brief mit einem freundlichen und höflichen Satz ab.

  Beispiele:
  I hope that you are able to help me. (wenn du um Hilfe oder einen Gefallen bittest)
  I hope that I have answered your question clearly. (wenn du auf eine Anfrage antwortest)
  I look forward to hearing from you. (wenn du möchtest, dass dir jemand antwortet)

Exercise 3 Write one sentence to start your letter using the following information:

a) price / ticket / Rock in Park concert
   I would like to know the price …
b) (*to a shop*) complain / new camera / last week
c) visit London / February / information / accommodation
d) (*reply to*) advert / cheap flights / Dublin / information
e) (*reply to*) Mrs Davy's letter / 6/10/2004

Exercise 4 Which endings would be best for the following situations:

1 You have complained to a shop.
2 You're trying to find a present.
3 You've invited your penfriend to stay.
4 You want some information from a hotel.
5 Someone has asked you a question.

A Please let me know if you can come.
B I hope the problem can be solved quickly.
C I look forward to hearing from you.
D I hope I have answered your question.
E I hope that you can help me.

1	2	3	4	5

Exercise 5 Write one formal and one informal letter using the information provided. You may need to add some details yourself.

a) (*your address*) 67 West Heath Road, Reading, R61 TH9
an English project – Druids and Stonehenge – information, photos.
brochures – history – Stonehenge?
find out: why built – where stones from – how put into place.
2 photos: stone circle – stones compared to people
thanks for help – information.
The English Tourist Board, Dundee Avenue, London, W13 5WS

b) Today is 3rd August. You've been busy at school and have not written to your friend for a long time. You want to go camping in Scotland at Easter. You got a new tent for your birthday and have all the equipment but your parents will not allow you to go by yourself. Your friend always wanted to go to Scotland, too. Write to your friend about this. Your father will drive you both to Oban, in Scotland. If camping is no fun, you can always stay at youth hostels. You want to know for certain if your friend wants to come so explain that you will telephone on Sunday. Your address is: 23 High Street, Salthouse, NW34 6RT.

Leserbrief

- Ein Leserbrief beginnt normalerweise mit *'Dear Editor'* und endet mit *'Yours faithfully'*.
- Du kannst Kurzformen verwenden, aber sonst gelten die Regeln für den formellen Brief.
- In der Regel wird eine Ansicht oder eine persönliche Meinung deutlich ausgedrückt.
- Bedenke vorher den Ton, in dem du den Brief abfassen möchtest: kritisch, humorvoll, ironisch, positiv …
- Drücke dich präzise aus und komme schnell zum eigentlichen Punkt.
- Der Schluss fasst oft die Botschaft des Briefes in einem Satz zusammen (siehe Exercise 6).

Exercise 6 Write to a newspaper in reply to Mr George's letter of 23rd June. What comments could you make concerning the points he mentions? Make notes next to Mr George's letter as you are reading it. Write in the order that points arise. You will need to add further details for the letter layout yourself.

Background: An airport is going to be built near the town in which you live. The airport will take middle-sized planes and will be used a lot for holiday flights. The next nearest airport is Stanstead, a major international one, about 60 miles away. Many new jobs will be created and money will come into the town but there will be planes flying quite low over it. And, of course, an increase in road traffic.

true – but some are temporary and may not be from the area, e.g. builders

Dear Editor,
Why are people in this town so angry about the new airport? We have high unemployment here and this will bring many new jobs into the area. Workers will be needed to build it and once it's finished there will be many more permanent jobs from cleaners to secretaries, from airport staff to taxi drivers.
You'll no longer have to drive ninety minutes to Stanstead, with traffic jams and expensive parking. From our little town you'll be able to fly direct to all the major cities in Europe.
Of course, a few planes will need to fly above us but this will only affect the industrial areas in the east and a few people in the west: a small price to pay to secure the future of our town.
I say build the airport. Bring jobs to the town.
Yours faithfully,
Harry George

Exercise 7 Look carefully at the scene of the street musicians. Write observations about it in note form next to the photograph. These comments may be useful later.
violin – *Geige*, cello – *Cello*, double bass – *Kontrabaß*, bow – *Geigenbogen*

Exercise 8 Using full sentences, provide as much information as possible about the photograph.

a) Describe the street musicians.
b) What type of music do you think they are playing? Do they sing as well?
c) What are they selling and how are they doing this?
d) Where exactly are they playing?
e) What are the advantages and disadvantages of where they are playing?

Exercise 9 a) You are a member of the group and need to get permission to play in the street. Here are the notes that you have already made. You will need to add some further details.
(*write to*) Mr Brown, Room 6, The Council Offices, The Town Hall, Cambridge, CA9 PE32. / apply for music licence/ Cambridge town centre / the group's size / Boots the Chemist / 6/8/04 / 2x 30 minutes / OK to sell CDs? / licence cost? / how, where to pay?

b) You are an old person and angry about street musicians in Cambridge. You decide to write to the editor of the local newspaper. Consider carefully your arguments.

c) You were visiting Cambridge and saw the street musicians, who were very good and also very amusing. They attracted a large audience. Write to your friend Jenny, who lives in Germany, to tell her about what happened. Mention, for example, what you were doing and where the band was, describe them, their music and the audience. You will need to add some details for the layout yourself.

3 E-Mails

E-Mails sind normalerweise weniger förmlich als Briefe.

- Persönliche E-Mails sind wie geschriebene Unterhaltungen. Sie enthalten Kurzformen, leichte Grammatik, Füllwörter, Verallgemeinerungen, persönliche Meinungen ...
- Formelle E-Mails sollten dem Stil formeller Briefe folgen.
- Du solltest den Inhalt formeller E-Mails so kurz und präzise wie möglich halten.
- Du solltest auf E-Mails in dem Stil antworten, in dem die Person an dich geschrieben hat.
  Beispiele:
  Dear Ms Smith – Best wishes, John Dunn
  Dear Mr Dunn – Best wishes, Mandy Smith
  Dear Mike – Jane
  Dear Jane – Mike
- Da E-Mails gewöhnlich weniger förmlich sind als Briefe, sind '*Best wishes*' oder '*Kind regards*' passendere Schlussformeln. Persönliche E-Mails können auch nur mit dem Namen schließen. (Beachte: Viele E-Mails haben heute weder Anrede noch Schluss.)
- Gib immer einen passenden Betreff an, damit der Empfänger weiß, worum es in deiner E-Mail geht.

Exercise 10 You would like to have a summer holiday job and have seen this advert in 'BritMag'. Contact the hotel by e-mail showing your interest, giving a few details about yourself, the dates when you can work, and anything else that you feel is necessary.

Holiday Jobs

Required for summer: students to work in our busy hotel.
No experience necessary – good pay – bad hours!
Contact: Jenny Weston weshotel@dev.uk

Exercise 11 Here is the reply about your holiday job:

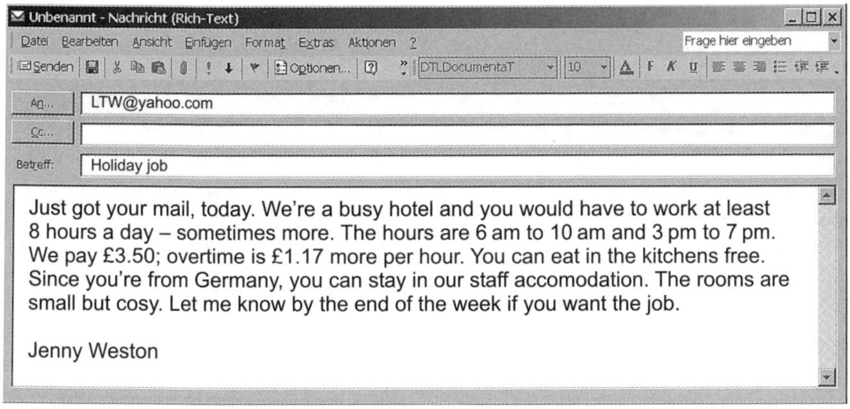

An: LTW@yahoo.com

Betreff: Holiday job

Just got your mail, today. We're a busy hotel and you would have to work at least 8 hours a day – sometimes more. The hours are 6 am to 10 am and 3 pm to 7 pm. We pay £3.50; overtime is £1.17 more per hour. You can eat in the kitchens free. Since you're from Germany, you can stay in our staff accomodation. The rooms are small but cosy. Let me know by the end of the week if you want the job.

Jenny Weston

You have written straight back to accept the job but now you want to tell your friend about it. Write a suitable e-mail.

Exercise 12 You ordered a book about England to take with you when you go on your holiday job. Unfortunately there is some bad news about it.

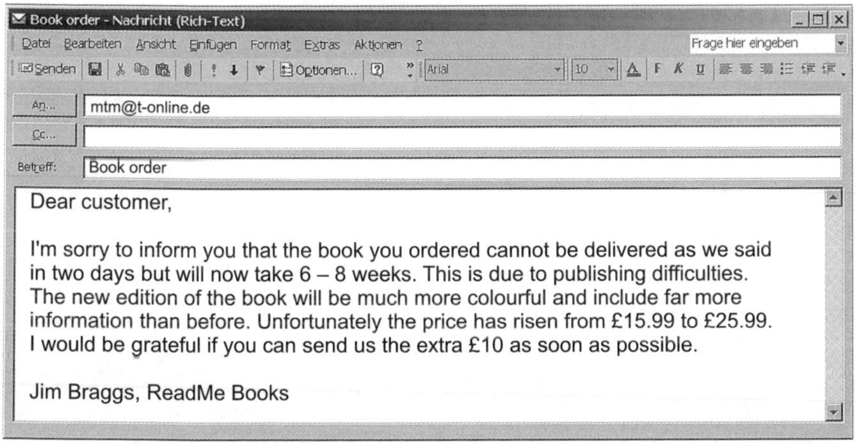

An: mtm@t-online.de

Betreff: Book order

Dear customer,

I'm sorry to inform you that the book you ordered cannot be delivered as we said in two days but will now take 6 – 8 weeks. This is due to publishing difficulties. The new edition of the book will be much more colourful and include far more information than before. Unfortunately the price has risen from £15.99 to £25.99. I would be grateful if you can send us the extra £10 as soon as possible.

Jim Braggs, ReadMe Books

Naturally, you are unhappy about this. In five weeks you are in England and you do not want to pay the extra money. What action will you take? Reply to the e-mail.

Visuelle Schreibimpulse • *Visual material*

Wenn du anhand eines Bildes einen Text verfassen sollst, so werden von dir in der Regel drei Bearbeitungsebenen verlangt:

- Analyse: Identifizierung der einzelnen Teile des Bildes
- Beschreibung: Du musst so über das Bild schreiben, als ob du es jemandem erklärst, der es nicht sehen kann.
- Interpretation: Was bedeutet das Bild und was sagt es aus?

Für die Bearbeitung der Aufgaben zur Bildanalyse, -beschreibung bzw. -interpretation ist es hilfreich, wenn du im Bild Anmerkungen (z. B. durch Einkreisen oder Pfeile) machst und anschließend stichwortartige Notizen anfertigst. Deine Anmerkungen im Bild und deine Notizen kannst du dann leicht in einen ausformulierten Aufsatz umwandeln.

1 Fotos

Ein Foto vermittelt ein unmittelbares Bild von einer Situation. Der Betrachter muss die Informationen, die es liefert, herausfinden und interpretieren. Daher musst du lernen,

- genau hinzusehen und Details zu untersuchen,
- die Gründe herauszufinden, aus denen ein Foto gemacht worden ist,
- den Unterschied zwischen Analyse, Beschreibung und Interpretation zu erkennen.

Analyse (*analysing*)

- Was kannst du sehen?
- Gibt es wichtige Informationen im Hintergrund (z. B. Schilder, Uhren, Menschen)?
- Stelle dir selbst Fragen und versuche, sie zu beantworten (z. B. Warum lächelt jemand?).

Beschreibung (*describing*)

- Beschreibe das Foto so, als ob du es jemandem erklärtest, der es nicht sehen kann.
- Was für ein Thema wird gezeigt (z. B. Krieg oder Armut)?
- Werden Menschen gezeigt? Wenn ja: Wer sind sie, wo sind sie und was tun sie?

Details

- Schaue dir Gesichter, Hände, Kleidung und Gebäude an. Was sagen sie dir?
- Gibt es Hintergrunddetails, die dir weitere Informationen geben (z. B. eine Uhr, ein Ladenschild, Autos)?
- Jede Einzelheit könnte wichtig sein.

Interpretation

- Erzählt das Foto z. B. etwas über eine bestimmte Situation oder beleuchtet es ein Problem?
- Welche Schlüsse kannst du aus dem ziehen, was du siehst?
- Was tun die Menschen auf dem Foto und warum tun sie es?
- Warum wurde das Foto gemacht (soll es schockieren, informieren oder etwas enthüllen)?

Grammatik

Wenn du die Handlung beschreibst, die auf einem Foto festgehalten ist, solltest du die Verlaufsform verwenden.

Exercise 1 Look at the photograph carefully. Write notes about it. The arrows show you what to write about.

Exercise 2 Describe the following sections of the photograph in exercise 1:

a) the scene.

b) each of the children in detail.

Example: *The boy is wearing a peaked cap with a scarf covering most of his head. He is also wearing a checked shirt, black trousers and some type of loose jacket tied in the middle. He has his head bowed as if he is looking for something on the floor. The boy appears quite young, probably not even a teenager.*

Exercise 3 Answer the following questions by interpreting what you see in the photograph of the children:

a) Why are the children collecting things from the rubbish dump?

b) What does this tell you about the society in which they live?

c) Where do you think the photograph has been taken?

d) What are the children's lives like? Think about schools, adults, education, work, and homes, for example.

Exercise 4 Make notes about the photograph of the street scene.

Exercise 5 Describe in detail the photograph from exercise 4 using full sentences.

Exercise 6 Answer the following questions about the photograph of the street scene.

a) What images tell you where the photograph has been taken?

b) What type of area do you think the photograph shows?

c) Why do you think there are no white people in the photograph?

Exercise 7 Interpret the photograph in exercise 4. What does it tell you about Britain?

2 Cartoons

Es gibt viele verschiedene Arten von Karikaturen. In der Schule werden gewöhnlich Karikaturen aus Zeitungen verwendet, d. h. es handelt sich um politische Karikaturen oder um solche, die aktuelle Themen kommentieren. Von Fotos unterscheiden sie sich dadurch, dass jemand sie gezeichnet hat. Das bedeutet:

- Alles, was in der Karikatur dargestellt ist, hat eine ganz bestimmte Bedeutung.
- Der Karikaturist verfolgt ein bestimmtes Ziel und drückt seine persönlichen Gedanken aus.
- Der Karikaturist drückt eine weit verbreitete Meinung aus.

Analyse

- Identifiziere alles, was in der Karikatur dargestellt ist.
- Kommentiere so viele Details wie möglich (z. B. die Gesichter von Menschen, Kleidung, Schilder).
- Stelle dir Fragen zu den Menschen oder Gegenständen in der Karikatur und versuche, sie zu beantworten (z. B. Warum schläft der Hund?).
- Spielt Symbolik eine Rolle? Stehen Gegenstände für etwas anderes (z. B. eine Krone für die Monarchie)?

Beschreibung

- Gib so viele Informationen wie möglich.
- Beschreibe die Karikatur so, als ob du sie jemandem erklärst, der sie nicht sehen kann.
- Was ist dargestellt?
- Falls Menschen gezeigt werden: Wer sind sie und was tun sie?

Details

- Sieh dir Gesichter, Hände, Kleidung, Gebäude an. Was verraten sie dir?
- Gibt es Details im Hintergrund, die dir weitere Informationen liefern (z. B. eine Uhr, ein Ladenschild, ein Plakat oder Gebäude)?
- Nichts ist ohne Grund dargestellt. Versuche herauszufinden, was der Grund sein könnte.

Karikaturunterschriften / eingebaute Texte (*cartoon captions / embedded texts*)

- Eine Karikaturunterschrift ist ein Kommentar, der unter der Karikatur steht. Sie kann z. B. Worte oder Gedanken einer Figur in der Karikatur ausdrücken.
- Unter eingebauten Texten versteht man alles Geschriebene in der Karikatur (z. B. Sprechblasen oder Wandplakate).
- Wer spricht mit wem?
- Welche Bedeutung haben die Aussagen?
- Verwendet der Karikaturist Wortspiele? Wenn ja: Was will er sagen?

Interpretation

- Wovon handelt die Karikatur? Kommentiert sie eine Situation? Wie lautet die Botschaft?
- Was für eine Karikatur ist es (z. B. ein politischer Kommentar oder ein Angriff auf die Monarchie)?
- Warum hat der Karikaturist dieses Thema gewählt? Ist es aktuell, will er eine weit verbreitete Meinung ausdrücken, will er schockieren, informieren oder etwas näher beleuchten?
- Erfüllt die Karikatur ihren Zweck?

Grammatik

Wenn du die in einer Karikatur festgehaltene Handlung beschreibst, solltest du die Verlaufsform verwenden.

Exercise 8 Study the cartoon carefully, then make notes about it.

Exercise 9 Describe the cartoon in exercise 8 in full sentences.

Exercise 10 Answer the following questions about the Olympic Games cartoon.

a) Why is the British team unhappy?

b) Why are the Americans and the Chinese happy?

c) Why 'London 2012'?

d) Why are there embedded texts and explain what they mean?

Exercise 11 Interpret the cartoon from exercise 8 in approximately 100 words.

Exercise 12 Analyse the cartoon "Please – no Brits!!" in note form.

Please - no Brits!!

Exercise 13 Describe the scene in the cartoon "Please – no Brits!!".

Exercise 14 Interpret the cartoon in exercise 12 and explain the caption.

3 Bilder und Gemälde

Für alles, was auf einem Bild dargestellt ist, gibt es einen Grund. Du benötigst keine großen Kunstkenntnisse, um Beobachtungen zu machen. Eventuell musst du zu einem Bild eine Geschichte erfinden. Daher solltest du dir das Bild ganz genau ansehen, bevor du es beschreibst und analysierst.

Analyse

- Mache dir Notizen zu dem Bild, benutze Pfeile, um die entsprechenden Teile zu kennzeichnen.
- Sieh dir jeden Teil des Bildes genau an.
- Kommentiere Einzelheiten (z. B. die Blickrichtung der Personen, ihren Gesichtsausdruck, ihre Kleidung, Gebäude).

Beobachtung

- Was geschieht auf dem Bild?
- Was sagt uns der Künstler über die Szene?
- Welche soziale Stellung haben die Menschen? Sind sie reich oder arm?
- Wer oder was steht im Mittelpunkt des Bildes? Warum?
- Wie ist die Atmosphäre? Ist sie z. B. angespannt, entspannt, humorvoll oder bedrohlich?
- Um was für eine Art von Gemälde handelt es sich? Erzählt es eine Geschichte? Ist z. B. ein historisches Ereignis, eine Alltagsszene oder politische Propaganda dargestellt?
- Sieh dir sorgfältig Gesichtsausdrücke, Hände und Körpersprache der dargestellten Personen an.
- Überlege, was dir bestimmte Gegenstände sagen können. Warum hält z. B. jemand einen Brief in der Hand? Was sagen uns die Reihen von Büchern im Hintergrund eines Porträts über die dargestellte Person?

Beschreibung

- Beschreibe den allgemeinen Schauplatz, als ob du jemandem davon erzählst, der ihn nicht sehen kann.
- Beschreibe Details in Bezug auf die Personen, ihre Kleidung und ihre Körpersprache.
- Sieh dir den Hintergrund an und erkläre, warum der Künstler ihn gewählt hat.
- Wird durch Lichteffekte eine besondere Atmosphäre geschaffen?
- Wird durch die Anordnung von Personen oder Gegenständen ein Spannungsverhältnis aufgebaut?

Grammatik

Wenn du die in einem Gemälde festgehaltene Handlung beschreibst, solltest du die Verlaufsform verwenden.

Exercise 15 Look carefully at Lowry's painting. Make notes about what you can see.

Exercise 16 a) How observant are you? Be as accurate as possible. Answer either *yes* or *no* to the following statements about Lowry's painting.

	Yes	No
There is a house in the background.	☐	☐
The men are working class.	☐	☐
Two people are fighting.	☐	☐
It is summer.	☐	☐
The street is somewhere in America.	☐	☐
The people are all wearing expensive clothes.	☐	☐
The scene is less than fifty years ago.	☐	☐
Most people are old.	☐	☐

The cheapest room is 4d.	☐	☐
The light stops the window looking empty.	☐	☐
There are two dogs on the pavement.	☐	☐
The dogs are scared of the fighting.	☐	☐

b) Using complete sentences, explain the reason for each of the answers you gave in exercise a.

For example:
(no) The building in the background is a cheap guesthouse; the prices are in the window.

Exercise 17 Describe Lowry's painting as if you were on the phone telling someone about it.

Vorstellungsvermögen und Kreativität

Häufig werden von dir Einfallsreichtum und Kreativität im Zusammenhang mit der Beschreibung und Analyse von Gemälden verlangt. Dann musst du Folgendes näher betrachten:

- Welche Ereignisse sind dargestellt?
- Welche Epoche ist dargestellt?
- Welche Personen sind dargestellt? Welchen Charakter haben sie und wie reagieren sie?
- Wie könnte man den Text interessant gestalten (z. B. durch das Hinzufügen von Einzelheiten, das Aufbauen von Spannung, durch eine abwechslungsreiche Sprache)?
- Wie könnte man Dialoge erstellen?

Exercise 18 Write a dialogue between *either* two of the people in Lowry's picture, exercise 15, *or* the woman on the right and a friend she meets later. You may wish to look at the notes on pages 5–11 about dialogues.

Exercise 19 Write a short article for a local newspaper about what happened. You may wish to look at the notes on pages 57–61 about writing newspaper articles.

Exercise 20 Continue the story about the incident by writing another 150 words. You are the person standing at the door entrance.

I was about to leave the guesthouse to look for a much needed job when I heard voices. It wasn't unusual to hear people at this time of day in the street outside but unusual to hear such loud and angry ones …

4 Diagramme

Grafische Darstellungen geben einen visuellen Überblick über eine Situation. Einzelheiten werden in einem leicht verständlichen Format dargestellt. Da der Informationsgehalt häufig aber sehr hoch ist, musst du Schaubilder, Diagramme, Grafiken und Statistiken sehr genau betrachten und analysieren.

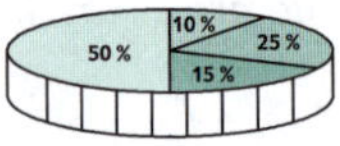

pie chart

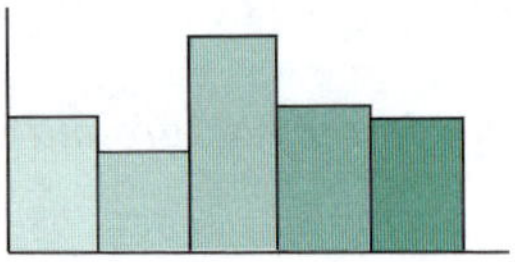
bar chart

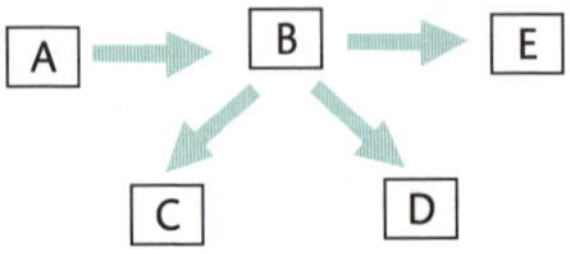

flow chart

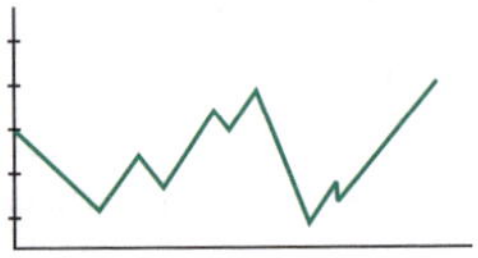
graph

Andere nützliche Wörter:
table – eine Tabelle, normalerweise in Reihen oder Spalten
row – eine waagerechte Tabellenzeile
column – eine senkrechte Tabellenspalte
heading – Titel
labeling – Beschriftung eines Diagramms

Informationen lesen

- Schlage unbekannte Wörter nach: Informationen in Schaubildern sind oft sehr verdichtet und du musst jedes Wort verstehen.
- Hast du die Informationen, die das Schaubild vermittelt, in der richtigen Reihenfolge gelesen?
- Was ist der Zweck des Schaubildes?

Zeichnungen und Fotos analysieren

- Wenn du dir Notizen zu den Illustrationen und Fotos machst, kann dir das helfen, sie besser zu verstehen. Stelle dir zu den Bildern Fragen (z. B. Warum sind sie da? Welchen Zweck haben sie? Was genau zeigen die Bilder?).
- Lerne, die Bilder in allen Einzelheiten zu beschreiben.
- Enthalten die Bilder zusätzliche Informationen, die du für das Verständnis des Schaubildes brauchst?

Auswertung von Statistiken (*interpreting statistics*)

- Wie wird das statistische Material präsentiert (z. B. als Tabelle, Säulendiagramm)?
- Was zeigt die Statistik?
- Lerne, Statistiken auf unterschiedliche Weise zu analysieren und herauszufinden, welcher Schwerpunkt für deine Argumentation wichtig ist.

Beispiel: (statistic) Approximately 10 % of young people believe nuclear power to be the most important green issue.
(negative interpretation) Most young people do not believe nuclear power to be the main green issue.
(positive interpretation) One in ten of 15- to 20-year olds consider nuclear power to be the most important green issue.

Beschreibung

Beschreibe grafische Darstellungen so, als ob du sie jemandem erklärtest, der sie nicht sehen kann.

Exercise 21 Some difficult words have been selected from the diagram in exercise 22. Connect each word to its meaning.

1 welfare	A pollution from cars and other vehicles
2 set	B earth / ground
3 issues	C pollution
4 exhaust emissions	D care
5 GM	E points
6 soil	F group / collection
7 contamination	G genetically modified

1	2	3	4	5	6	7

Exercise 22 Look carefully at the survey diagram. Answer the following questions:

a) What is the diagram about?
b) How is the information presented?
c) Analyse the background picture.
d) Write a positive interpretation of the global warming statistic.
e) Write a negative interpretation of the water pollution statistic.

In a survey, 15- to 21-year olds were asked:
Animal welfare in farming and science is often seen as part of a wider set of policies for the environment. From this list of "green" issues, which would you say was the most important to you?

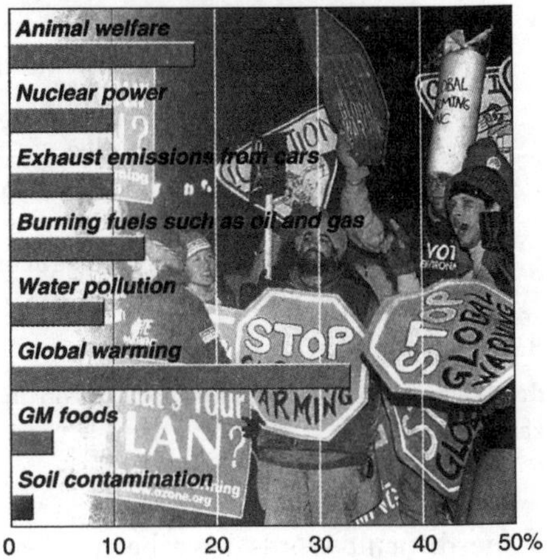

Exercise 23 Write an analysis of the information in the diagram of the survey.

Exercise 24 What is your reaction to the survey results about young people's opinions concerning the environment? Write about 100 words.

Exercise 25 Look carefully at the diagram below. Check any unknown words in a dictionary.

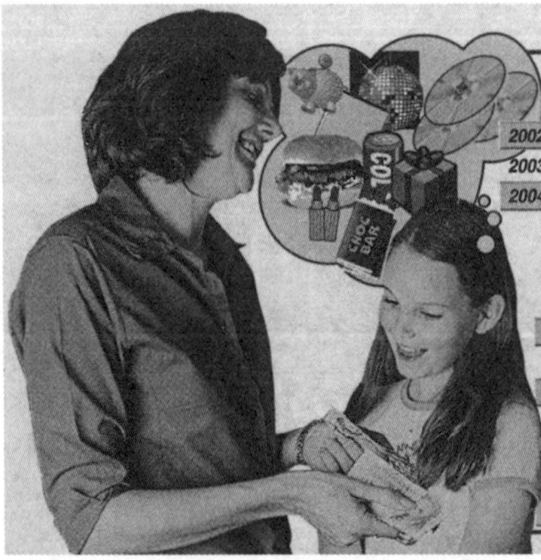

WHAT CHILDREN WILL GET

	Population aged 7-16	Weekly amount	Annual total
2002	7.76m	£6.73	£2.72bn
2003	7.72m	£6.80	£2.73bn
2004	7.69m	£7.10	£2.84bn
2005	7.62m	£7.40	£2.93bn
2006	7.58m	£7.73	£3.05bn

Source: Mintel

... AND WHERE IT GOES

Percentage of children who spend their money on these products

	Boys	Girls
Toys/games	70%	52%
Crisps/sweets	58%	58%
Computer/video games	50%	14%
Drinks	34%	32%
Magazines/comics	32%	39%
Books	30%	44%
Presents for people	23%	35%
Sports/hobbies	23%	10%
Records/tapes/CDs	22%	43%
Savings	18%	26%
Going out	15%	19%
Clothes	13%	39%
Toiletries/cosmetics	1%	13%

Source: TGI Youth survey

a) Describe the diagram and explain what it is showing?

b) Which of the following statements about the diagram are *true* and which are *false*?

	true	false
There will be fewer 7- to16-year olds in the future.	☐	☐
Since 2002, the amount of money 7- to16-year olds can spend is getting smaller.	☐	☐
There is little difference in what boys and girls spend their money on.	☐	☐
Girls are more likely to buy music to listen to than boys.	☐	☐
Most young people spend their money on toys and games.	☐	☐
Boys spend one third less on clothes than girls.	☐	☐
Boys do not go out very much and like to save their money.	☐	☐
Girls and boys have similar interests.	☐	☐
Boys prefer sport to smelling nice!	☐	☐

c) Interpret the statistics in the diagram. What can you say about them and what do they show?
Consider:

- trends and the future
- differences between boys and girls
- spending power
- what they say about our society
- what they mean to businesses

Zeitungsartikel • *Newspaper articles*

Wenn du einen Zeitungsartikel verfassen möchtest, musst du Folgendes beachten:

- Dein Artikel muss detaillierte Informationen enthalten.
- Du solltest den Text interessant und leicht verständlich gestalten.
- Du solltest nur wichtige Informationen vermitteln und unwichtige Einzelheiten oder Wiederholungen vermeiden.

Es gibt einige Stilmittel, die dir helfen können, deinen Schreibstil beim Abfassen von Zeitungsberichten und Zeitungsartikeln zu verbessern.

Alliteration *(alliteration)*

Bei Überschriften von Zeitungsartikeln kann es sehr wirkungsvoll sein, wenn du sie aus mehreren Wörtern mit demselben Anfangsbuchstaben zusammensetzt.

Beispiel: Cambridge chaos.

Rhetorische Frage *(rhetorical question)*

Um z. B. die Leser deines Kommentars nachdenklich zu machen, eignen sich rhetorische Fragen sehr gut: Du stellst hierfür einfach eine oder mehrere (provozierende) Fragen, die du nicht direkt beantwortest.

Beispiel: Why shouldn't we have the freedom to choose?

Ton *(tone)*

Auch in einem Zeitungsartikel musst du deine Worte sehr sorgfältig wählen. Deine Wortwahl ist entscheidend dafür, ob dein Text sachlich, kritisch oder unterstützend klingt.

Beispiele: The captain took the boat out to sea. (factual)
The captain foolishly took the boat out to sea. (critical)
The captain bravely took the boat out to sea. (supportive)

Satzlänge *(sentence length)*

Kurze Sätze betonen, was du sagen willst, und lenken die Aufmerksamkeit auf eine bestimmte Tatsache. Lange Sätze ermöglichen es dir hingegen, Einzelheiten zu nennen und zu beschreiben. Setze lange und kurze Sätze ganz bewusst als Stilmittel ein.

Beispiele: Six people escaped.
Flames appeared from every entrance making it impossible for the firemen to get any closer to the inferno, then suddenly a window broke and six people jumped clear of the burning building.

Exercise 1 Write a suitable headline for each of the following themes. Where possible use alliteration.

a) A lot of very bad driving on the motorway caused many accidents in poor weather conditions.

b) A local businessman, Harry Mann, has just given a very large amount of money to a local charity to help handicapped children.

c) A factory, which has always made your town look ugly, has been rebuilt.

d) A bad storm during the night damaged many buildings and caused problems everywhere.

e) A snake has escaped from a local zoo. It is harmless but it is very big and could give people a shock if they meet it.

f) Someone has stolen Edward Munch's famous painting *The Scream* from a gallery where it was on special loan for an exhibition.

Exercise 2 Using the style of a newspaper reporter, write a few sentences including a rhetorical question concerning each statement. You can choose to agree or disagree with the statement.

a) Students do not do enough work at school and should learn more.
Example:
Students do work hard at school. They are constantly having to write tests, do homework and prepare for lessons. Isn't that enough? (disagreeing)

b) Young people today are only interested in having fun not hard work.

c) Smoking should be banned from all public places.

d) Shops are open on Sundays.

e) People should be more willing to move around the country and from country to country in their search for employment.

Exercise 3 Change each sentence so that it has a critical tone and then a supportive one.

a) Europe is going ahead with its space rocket programme.
Europe is going ahead with its unnecessary and expensive space rocket programme. (critical)
Europe, at last, is going ahead with its space rocket programme. (supportive)

b) Cloning is the way forward for medicine.

c) The EU will get much larger.

d) Young people spend a lot of time with computers today.

Exercise 4 Write the following sentences more concisely.

a) It was not long before there was running and screaming everywhere.
Suddenly, there was chaos everywhere.

b) The strike resulted in many passengers having to wait a long time on cold platforms for their trains.

c) The accident between the red BMW and the green Opel happened at the corner of St. James's Street in the town centre.

d) When the French President arrived at the new building on his official visit to open it, there were many people who had come from a long way to watch the event and welcome him.

Exercise 5 Write a text of between 120–180 words about the photograph varying the length of your sentences and adopting a suitable tone. If you cannot think of your own theme or headline use one of the following suggestions: *severe storms leave coastal chaos; rotting wreck litters beach; remove it!*

Ein Zeitungsartikel sollte aus vier Teilen bestehen:

- einer guten Schlagzeile,
- einer Einleitung,
- einem Hauptteil mit Einzelheiten,
- einem Schluss / einer Schlussfolgerung.

Schlagzeile (*headline*)

- Sie sollte die Aufmerksamkeit des Lesers erregen.
- Wortspiele und Alliterationen sind wichtige Bestandteile einer Schlagzeile.
- Es ist oft einfacher, zuerst den Artikel zu schreiben und dann die Schlagzeile zu verfassen.

Einleitung (*introduction*)

- Fasse die Situation unter folgenden Gesichtspunkten zusammen und halte die Einzelheiten so knapp wie möglich: Wer war beteiligt? Was geschah? Wo geschah es? Wann geschah es?

  Beispiel: Yesterday, the Prime Minister's car was attacked by demonstrators as he left No. 10 Downing Street.

Hauptteil *(main part)*

- Erweitere die Geschichte durch zusätzliche Informationen.
- Ordne die Ereignisse nach ihrer zeitlichen Abfolge.
- Ordne die Argumente logisch.
- Baue Zitate ein, falls erforderlich.

Schluss *(ending)*

- Haben die Ereignisse Konsequenzen oder gibt es Ergebnisse?
- Ist bei dem Text, den du schreibst, eine persönlich gehaltene Zusammenfassung oder ein Kommentar nötig?

  Beispiele: After the attack on the Prime Minister's car security is to be tightened.
  It is necessary after the shameful attack on the PM's car to tighten up security.

Stil *(style)*

Was für einen Artikel schreibst du?

- Tatsachenberichte geben objektiv Einzelheiten wieder, ohne dass der Verfasser Stellung bezieht.
- Leitartikel geben die Meinung der Zeitung (des Chefredakteurs) zu einer bestimmten Situation wieder.
- Objektive Artikel stellen die Tatsachen unbeeinflusst dar, alle Seiten sollten gleich behandelt werden, ohne dass eine persönliche Meinung ausgedrückt wird.
- Subjektive Artikel geben die Meinung einer Person wieder, ohne dass andere, abweichende Ansichten erwähnt werden.

Vorgehensweise beim Schreiben von Artikeln

- Bevor du anfängst zu schreiben, solltest du Stichpunkte notieren zu dem, was du sagen möchtest, und zu den Einzelheiten, die du anführen möchtest.
- Entscheide, welche Informationen in die Einleitung, in den Mittelteil und in den Schluss gehören.
- Ordne deine Punkte logisch.
- Schreibe präzise und klar.

Exercise 6 Write the first line of an article based on the following topics. Remember to write concisely and use the *who*, *what*, *where* and *when* approach.

a) The American President arrived to talk to the British Prime Minister.

b) Football hooligans.

c) A pop concert.

d) A demonstration against a planned motorway.

Exercise 7 Write a short article about the rhinoceros escaping. Include a good headline, some stylistic devices, vary the length of your sentences and adopt a suitable tone. Make notes before you begin.

headline	→	**introduction:** *who, what, where, when*	→	**middle section:** *details*	→	**ending:** *summary conclusion comment*

Exercise 8 Read the information about the Titanic disaster. Check any unknown words in a dictionary before you start the exercises.

The Titanic

The Titanic was the most elegant ship in the world at the time and considered unsinkable due to its construction. However, the events leading up to the Titanic tragedy had already begun unknowingly before it had even left Southampton harbour, when a decision was made shortly before sailing to remove half of the lifeboats onboard to make more room on deck for the passengers to walk about. Around midday, 10th April 1912 the largest luxury liner of the White Star Line Company set off for America among much publicity.

For three days all went well on the ship's first voyage but everything was to change very quickly during the night of 14th April. The ship was steaming at full speed for New York in calm Atlantic seas and although it had already received a number of warnings about icebergs the Titanic did not slow down. Shortly before midnight a mountainous iceberg was spotted directly in front of the ship. The crew tried to avoid the accident by reversing the engines but although they missed hitting the iceberg with the front of the ship, the ice tore a hole under the waterline along the length of it.

It did not take long before Captain Smith and the ship's designer, Thomas Andrew, who was also on board, realised that the ship was sinking very quickly and it could not be saved. The order was given to get everyone into the lifeboats and off the ship. But the terrible decision earlier to remove many of the lifeboats meant there were only enough for half the passengers. As people panicked the situation worsened and many of the lifeboats were launched only half full.

Sadly, there were many incidents of self-preservation later reported. There were stories of people refusing to turn their half-empty lifeboats back towards the sinking ship to pick up survivors from the water because they might become over full. Even the managing director of the White Star Line helped women and children into a lifeboat and then got in to save himself.

The captain made the hard decision that women and children should be first off the ship. This meant the men had to stay behind to face an almost certain death. In less than three hours the Titanic sank and from approximately 2,220 passengers only 705 survived. Although one ship, the California, was close to the Titanic's position when she sank, it did not respond to the emergency call over the radio and, therefore, many lives were lost which could, perhaps, have been saved.

a) It is 15th April 1912, you are just about to start printing the morning paper when you receive news of the disaster. Write a short factual article about it. Before you begin consider: this is late news and you do not have a lot of details. What do you know? Structure the article carefully. Make notes before you start writing.

b) Write an editorial column about one aspect of the Titanic disaster. For example, why ships are allowed to sail without enough lifeboats, safety at sea or people's responsibilities.

c) Imagine that you have just finished interviewing some of the survivors of the Titanic. Write an appropriate newspaper article giving their stories. Some areas you may wish to consider are, for example:
   - *Introduction*: who, what, where and when
   - *Middle section*: Who were the people? Where were they on the Titanic? When did they realise something was wrong? What happened next? How did they get off? What was the scene like and people's reactions? How and when did help arrive?
   - *Ending/conclusion*: about the construction of ships, safety aspects, who is responsible? What happens to the survivors?

d) Provide three good headings for your articles.

Exercise 9 Give two concise and factual reports on current news topics. In both cases limit what you write to a maximum of 250 words.

Exercise 10 Vocabulary: there are some words which you should know concerning newspapers and their contents. Look carefully at the clues and see if you can give the correct words, which have been jumbled up.

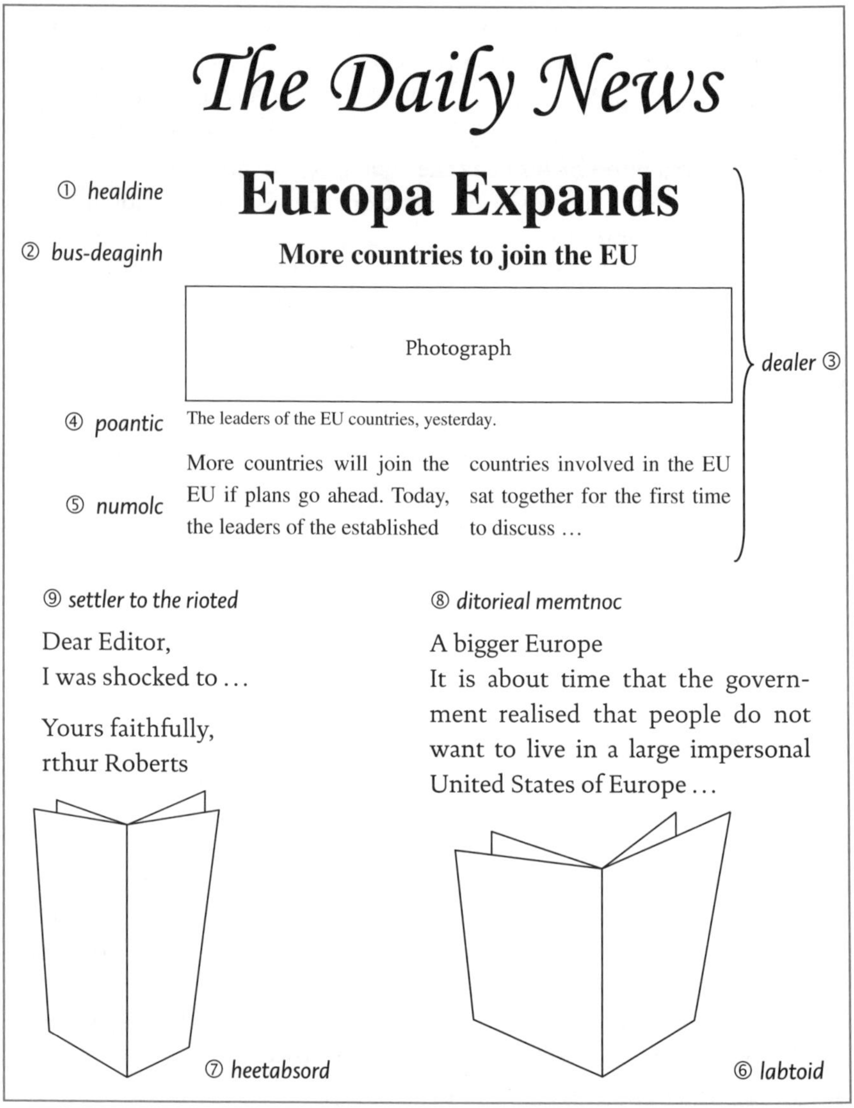

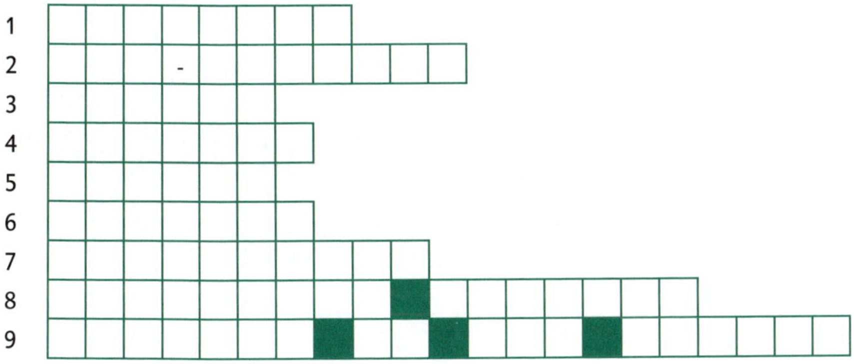

Note: Many broadsheet newspapers, for example The Times and The Independent, are now printing their newspapers in the form of a tabloid. However they are not called tabloids, instead they are called 'compact newspapers'.

Kreatives Schreiben • *Creative writing*

Kreativ schreiben heißt, dass du in der Lage sein musst, dir Situationen und Charaktere vorzustellen und gleichzeitig das Interesse des Lesers zu wecken. Es ist wichtig, dass du keine oberflächlichen, einfachen Geschichten ohne Inhalt schreibst. Du solltest

- Einzelheiten über Schauplätze und Gefühle hinzufügen,
- mehr als nur ein Geschichtenerzähler sein und dich aktiv an der Situation beteiligt fühlen,
- persönliche Erfahrungen und Menschen, die du kennst, einbauen,
- auf deine eigenen Erfahrungen mit Gefühlen zurückgreifen, z. B. Trauer, Freude, Einsamkeit, Langeweile.

Bevor du anfängst zu schreiben, solltest du planen, was du schreiben willst:

- Welche Ideen hast du?
- Wer sind die Charaktere?
- Wie sieht der Handlungsverlauf aus?
- Möchtest du Dialoge einbauen?
- Wo spielt die Handlung?
- Welche Absicht verfolgst du?

Ideen

- Welche Art von Text soll es sein: dramatisch, beschreibend, humorvoll, ein Text mit oder ohne Dialog oder nur ein Dialog?
- Aus welchem Blickwinkel willst du den Text schreiben?
- Vollziehen sich die Entwicklungen schnell oder langsam?
- Möchtest du ein „Was wäre, wenn …“-Szenario?
- Möchtest du eine Auflösung oder ein offenes Ende?
- Gibt es eine besondere Situation oder besondere Umstände?

Charaktere

- Wer sind sie?
- Fertige Charakteranalysen an (z. B. Aussehen, Auftreten, Verhalten, Gesellschaftsschicht, siehe S. 7–9).

Schauplatz (*setting*)

- Wo spielt die Handlung?
- Möchtest du eine besondere Atmosphäre schaffen? Wie kannst du sie beschreiben?
- Sind Menschen anwesend?

Handlungsablauf (*plot*)

- Was wird geschehen (z. B. ein Verbrechen, ein Unfall, das Treffen zweier Menschen)?
- Wer tut wem was?
- Wo und wann?

Absicht (*intention*)

- Was ist dein Ziel?
- Erzählst du eine Geschichte oder beschreibst du eine Person?
- Was sind die wichtigsten Aspekte (z. B. die Menschen, die Atmosphäre oder die Geschichte)?
- Welchen Stil möchtest du verwenden (z. B. Spannung, Humor, Sarkasmus)?

Notizen machen und „Mindmapping“

Sieh dir die einzelnen Punkte genau an und gliedere sie auf, um die besten Ideen zu bekommen.

Beispiel:

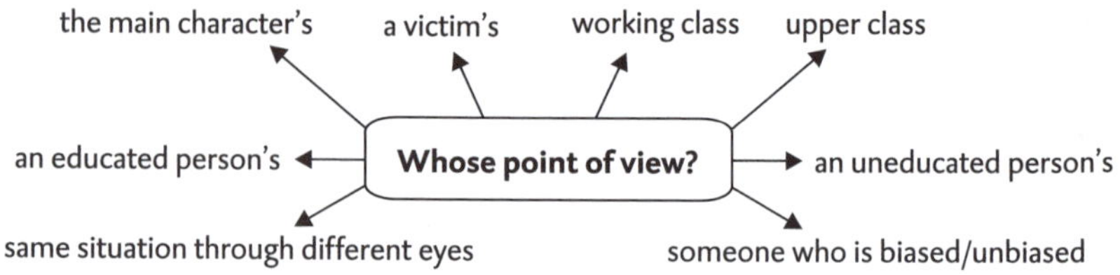

Exercise 1 Using the headings *ideas, characters, setting, plot* and *intention*, write notes about the following theme: *The demonstration.*

Example:

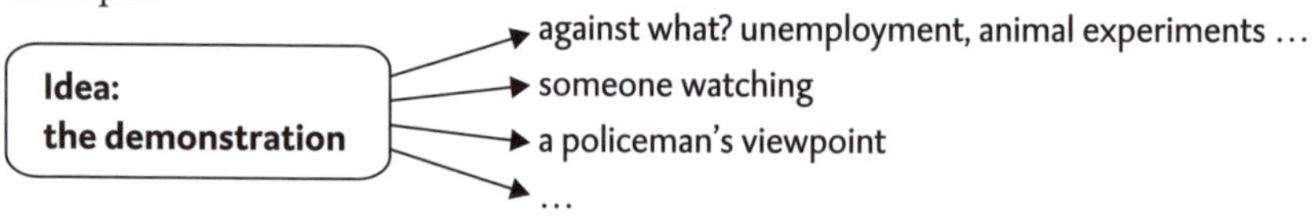

Exercise 2 Make character studies of the people below in note form. Then describe them in full sentences. (You may wish to look at pages 7–9 concerning how to write character studies.)

a) James: quiet and gentle

character	age	background	personality and behaviour	appearance
James	early 20s	educated, middle class	quiet, gentle, does not like angering people or hurting them but likes being with people	pleasant, clean, tidy, smart

James is one of those people who is always there but seldom says anything. He's young, in his early twenties, and well-dressed. It's not that he has nothing to say, he's had a good education, but he never likes to anger people or disagree with them. He would never hurt anyone.

b) Sue: friendly and happy

character	age	background	personality and behaviour	appearance

c) Tom: not very pleasant

character	age	background	personality and behaviour	appearance

d) a shop assistant

character	age	background	personality and behaviour	appearance

e) a taxi driver

character	age	background	personality and behaviour	appearance

Exercise 3 Describe the viewpoints that people can have: *strong, weak, biased, unbiased, radical* and *conservative*. How would this affect their characters? Imagine six different characters and write up to 50 words about each of them and their viewpoints.

Example: (someone with a strong viewpoint)
Jane holds a strong point of view on everything and always wants everyone to listen to her. She takes over conversations and people quickly get tired of her. She is quite lonely and has very few friends but does not understand why.

Exercise 4 Describe the following settings as interestingly and creatively as possible. Begin by making notes and marking the words or phrases you would like to later use. Write between 50–100 words.

a) a room full of people
Example:

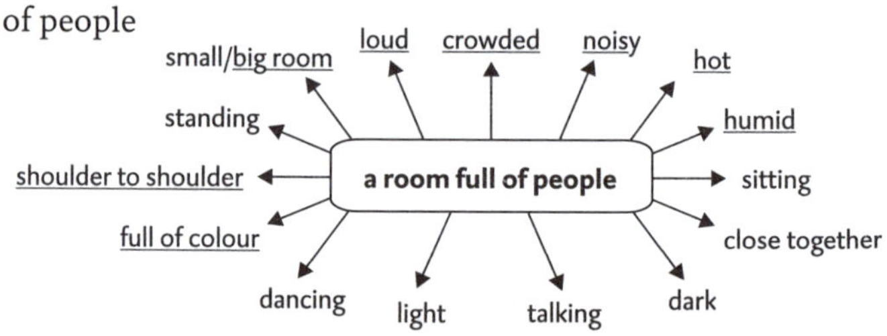

It was quite a big room but everywhere you looked there were people in it. It was loud and noisy, hot and humid. People were standing shoulder to shoulder, no room to turn or even make a little space for oneself. Individuals became a crowd and the crowd, if you looked down on it, was a moving carpet of colour.

60 words

b) a misty morning by the side of a river

c) inside a train

d) in a park

Ein Text besteht normalerweise aus
- einer Einleitung,
- einem Hauptteil mit Einzelheiten,
- einem Schluss.

Dein Text muss gut geplant sein, er muss korrigiert und eventuell noch einmal umgeschrieben werden.

Einleitung *(introduction)*

Es gibt keine Standardeinleitung, aber es gibt verschiedene Möglichkeiten für den Anfang:

- langsamer Anfang, die Szene vorbereiten

  Beispiel: It was some time in late autumn that Mike and Jenny decided to visit Aunt Miriam. They hadn't seen her for many years now and had changed a lot. Aunt Miriam was their mother's older sister who had left home when she was young to work abroad.

- beschreibender Anfang

  Beispiel: That particular late autumn was wonderful. The leaves were full of colour; golden browns, soft reds, greens and yellows. The warmth of the autumn shades was in contrast to the cold blue sky above. It was on such a day that Mike and Jenny decided to visit their old, adventurous Aunt Miriam who …

- dramatischer und plötzlicher Anfang

  Beispiel: "That's it! We're going! Aunt Miriam's been home for six months. It's now November and we haven't even seen her. She probably won't even recognise us." Jenny collected her bag, the flowers she'd bought for herself and joined Mike in the entrance.

Mittelteil *(middle section)*

- Erzähle die Geschichte und ihre Einzelheiten.
- Halte dich an ein eingegrenztes Thema. Wenn du zu viel einbaust, kann die Geschichte schnell oberflächlich werden.
- Verwende Stilmittel, die du kennst: Verändere z. B. die Satzlänge, baue Beschreibungen ein oder verwende nur *eine* Erzählperspektive.

Schluss oder Lösung *(ending/conclusion)*

- Der Schluss einer Geschichte kann eine Lösung beinhalten, es kann aber auch ein offenes Ende geben.
- Eine Lösung hält den Text zusammen. Sie fasst entweder das Geschriebene zusammen und beantwortet aufgeworfene Fragen oder sie drückt die Meinung des Schreibers zu einem Thema aus.
- Der Schluss oder die Lösung sollte für die Geschichte relevant sein.

Exercise 5 Write an introductory paragraph of less than 100 words to the topic "Snow chaos" and vary it in three different ways: slowly setting the scene, descriptively and dramatically.

Exercise 6 Write a middle section of a short story around each illustration. *Do not use dialogues* but be as creative as possible. You are given a start with which to build upon in two cases, in the last illustration you can develop your own ideas from the beginning.

a)

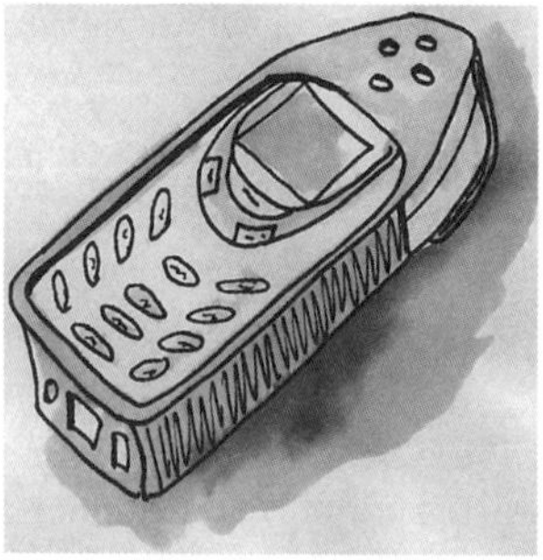

The mobile phone fell onto the stony path …

b)

So, this was the view that the prisoners had.

c)

Exercise 7 Build around each illustration a piece of creative writing which includes dialogue. In two cases you are given a starting point.

a) 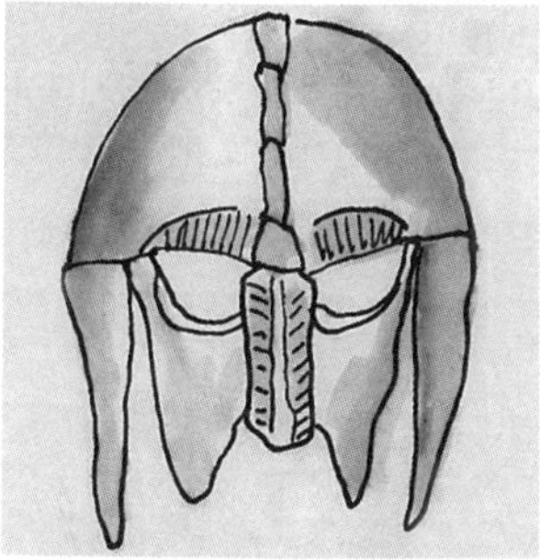

The builders were digging …

b) 

The bottle stood on the table, the message still inside it.

c) 

Exercise 8 Put three of the illustrations from exercises 6 and 7 in any order you wish and write a complete story about them with an introduction, a middle section and an ending. Dialogue can be included. Before you begin plan what you are going to write.

Exercise 9 Read the information carefully in preparation for a piece of creative writing.

Lord Tennyson wrote a famous poem called 'The Charge of the Light Brigade' which told the story of an event which happened on 25th October 1854 during the Crimean War. He wrote descriptively about the soldiers and the setting. For example,

'Their's not to reason why
Their's but to do and die'
'Cannon to the right of them,
Cannon to the left of them,
Cannon in front of them'.
(*here*, their's = their duty (job) is)

The British army faced a strong Russian one. The Russians, armed with cannons and with about 30,000 soldiers, held a strong position on both sides of a narrow valley. The Light Brigade, named because they were lightly armed with only swords and lances to fight with and rode fast horses, were told to attack a group of Russians on a hill which was away from the main area. The order was misunderstood and instead the soldiers, who numbered about 670, rode into the valley. In spite of the cannons firing all around them the Light Brigade did not turn back and rode on, breaking through those in front of them. With less that 200 survivors they attacked the huge Russian army which was waiting behind the cannons. Few returned.

a) Write an imaginary text around one aspect of the charge of the Light Brigade. Begin by deciding what type of text you want to write and what aspect you want to concentrate on.

Example:

The charge of the Light Brigade

- the atmosphere before
- a soldier's feelings
- watching and realising a mistake has happened
- family and friend's reactions afterwards
- a newspaper article: praise or critical?
- a survivor's story
- a Russian's viewpoint
- a wife's story
- …

Continue expanding your ideas. Think carefully, for example, about feelings, atmosphere, tragedy, bravery, or sadness. Imagine settings and how you can describe them.

b) Produce a piece of creative writing on the topic "The Charge of the Light Brigade". Write between 250–300 words.

Exercise 10

a) Study the illustration carefully. Make notes about it, for example describing the atmosphere, the café and the people.

b) Develop a piece of creative writing around the scene using between 200 – 300 words. You may, for example, take the role of one of the figures or be an observer, such as a waitress. What are the people discussing? Bring interest to the picture by adding tension, excitement or secrecy.

Exercise 11 Develop short stories around the following simple scenes. Begin by considering all the possible scenarios. Write between 200–300 words on each.

a) a twenty-pound note is lying on the pavement

Example:

a twenty-pound note is lying on the pavement

- who finds it? a tramp, his feelings?
- who lost it – rich /poor person, their reaction?
- when and where is the loss discovered?
- where is the money found? – a different country, a lonely street, a poor area, a rich area
- the note is an old one with Queen Victoria's face on it – strange, why?
- you read the next day about a robbery
- fantasy: the note has a life of its own. You try to pick it up but it moves / a dream with strange things happening

b) on the radio was her song

c) the forest path

d) a game

Wenn du einen guten kreativen Text schreiben möchtest, musst du durchlesen, was du geschrieben hast, und bereit sein, Teile zu ändern. Zu den allgemein üblichen Fehlern gehören

- unbeabsichtigte Wiederholungen,
- nicht präzise genug formulierte Punkte und Punkte ohne ausreichende Einzelheiten,
- schwache Formulierungen, Germanismen oder *false friends* (Ausdrücke, die in beiden Sprachen vorkommen, aber unterschiedliche Bedeutungen haben),
- Dialoge, die nicht realistisch klingen,
- Grammatik- und Inhaltsfehler.

Exercise 12 Rewrite the following sentences avoiding the repetitions by rewording sentences or using suitable synonyms.

a) Once inside the house the woman sat down. The woman wanted a rest from her busy day. The woman worked in a busy office.

b) Her shopping was heavy. She walked slowly with her heavy bag.

c) He looked down on the small boats in the harbour below. He never liked looking down. Flying made him scared and looking down always made him feel ill.

Exercise 13 Improve the following sentences by being more descriptive.

a) The girl walked to the bus stop.

b) It was a nice day. She got on her bike and rode it down the street.

c) There was a knock at the door. Tony answered it. When he got there, there was no one there.

Exercise 14 The underlined sections show some German expressions which are often wrongly included in English answers. Rewrite the sentences correctly.

a) She was a <u>sensible</u> child, always crying when things went wrong.

b) <u>In the last time</u> the house had been broken into many times.

c) <u>Actual</u> information about the robbery is difficult to get at the moment.

Exercise 15 Read the following dialogues carefully and then try to improve them by making them more realistic. Dialogues normally include short forms, imperatives and sometimes incomplete sentences.

a) "Look at that beautiful house in that lovely valley over there, David."
"I can see it, too. Yes, it is beautiful, it is really a very lovely house with a very big, pretty garden as well."

b) Tony said, "What was that terribly loud noise, Lucy?"
Lucy answered, "I do not know but I do not think it was anything to be scared about. Perhaps it was the wind."
Tony said, "I have never heard the wind make that type of noise. I am sure it was something breaking like glass or something similar."

Exercise 16 Explain what is wrong with the following sentences? How could you rewrite them?

a) Her silent footsteps were heard in the snow.

b) The storm was terrible. It was now the middle of the night and dark. The wind blew and the rain could be heard loudly against the windows.

c) Like a ghost, the black cat suddenly appeared on the high wall and then sprang, landing noisily on the soft grass below.

Präsentationen und Reden • *Presentations and speeches*

Es kann schwierig sein, Präsentationen und Reden zu halten, und bei einer Fremdsprache kommen noch zusätzliche Probleme hinzu. Folgenden Punkten solltest du daher besondere Aufmerksamkeit schenken:

- Sprache
- Geschwindigkeit des Vortrags
- deutliche Aussprache

Bei einer Präsentation vermittelst du Informationen, bei einer Rede machst du deinen Standpunkt zu einem Problem deutlich.

1 Präsentationen

Vorbereitung

- Notiere dir Stichpunkte zum Thema deiner Präsentation.
  Beispiel:

  book
  - details: author, title, …
  - concise introduction: novel/drama, topic …
  - summary of the plot
  - main characters
  - personal evaluation

- Wenn du viele Quellen benutzt, dann sammle die Informationen auf verschiedenen Blättern mit unterschiedlichen Überschriften, z. B. Einleitung, Zusammenfassung.

Wortschatz

- Verwende ein separates Handout für den Wortschatz: Liste die Vokabeln entweder in alphabetischer Reihenfolge auf oder in der Reihenfolge, in der die Wörter vorkommen. Mache deutlich, welche Methode du benutzt.
- Eine lange Vokabelliste ist abschreckend – begrenze die Liste auf etwa zehn Wörter. Wenn nötig, verwende Synonyme, um Ausdrücke in deiner Präsentation zu ersetzen.
- Spezialausdrücke solltest du während deiner Präsentation erklären.

Visuelle Hilfsmittel und Handouts

- Überprüfe deine Sprache und deine Rechtschreibung sorgfältig.
- Halte nur wichtige Punkte fest.
- Schreibe deutlich und präzise.
- Überlege, wie du Informationen vereinfachen kannst, z. B. ob du Stichpunkte wählst oder ganze Sätze.

Vortrag

- Aussprache: Kannst du alle Wörter korrekt aussprechen? Wenn nicht, kennst du ein passendes Synonym?
- Intonation: Du kannst bestimmte Punkte durch die Art und Weise, wie du sie sagst, hervorheben. Es ist langweilig, einer monotonen Stimme zuzuhören.
- Geschwindigkeit: Du darfst nicht zu langsam und vor allem nicht zu schnell sprechen. Du musst deutlich sprechen, damit deine Zuhörer dich verstehen können.
- Nimm deine Präsentation auf Kassette auf und höre sie dir dann an. Kannst du noch etwas verbessern?

Exercise 1 Imagine that the text is for a presentation. Read it through carefully.

The educated poor

How would you like to make the decision of going to university and being in debt for many years or getting a job?

Many English students wishing to study at university now face such a difficult decision. The opportunity of going to university was once one not to be missed. Not only did you become highly qualified, opening up top jobs but, at the same time, it was an opportunity to break away from home: to be responsible for yourself and your own finances. It was a transitional period between being dependent on parents and being independent.

A student's expectations were always high, to achieve academic success and gain a well-paid and interesting job, but debt is now included, too.

In the last twenty years there have been significant developments in government policies regarding further education. Going to university in the last ten years has frequently left students facing debts of £ 10,000 on average: money owed mainly to banks. Now universities are putting an extra burden on their students by charging fees of up to £ 2,500 per year. This additional cost means many first-year students will be faced with the prospect of leaving university with an estimated £ 20,000 debt. To put this into perspective this is less than a newly qualified teacher earns.

As a result, many students are applying to universities in their own areas trying to reduce costs by living with parents. Others are choosing not to go to uni-

versity for financial reasons. The current trend could also have consequences for courses studied. Should universities offer courses that are not job-orientated: education for education's sake, or should universities ensure that their courses have relevance for the job market?
Once students took courses that interested them. Now they need to consider which courses will provide the best opportunity for a future career, preferably with a high income, so that debts can be paid off. *316 words*

a) Write a vocabulary list of unknown words. Show the usage and give an alternative word or phrase if possible.

For example:

vocabulary	usage	alternative
debt	(to be) in debt	to owe money

b) Reduce the list of words to the ten most difficult.

c) Write a handout for a presentation using the text. Include only the main points but use full sentences.

For example:

The educated poor

English students face a choice: university and debt or getting a job.

d) What information would you include on a transparency? What phrases or key words would you use?

For example:

The educated poor

university and debts or working

...

Exercise 2 Before reading out loud anything you have prepared, mark pauses or things you wish to stress. Some suggestions are:

/ = a small pause

// = a longer pause, for example a full stop or the end of a paragraph

go = (underline) a word to stress

→ = phrases that need to be spoken together without pauses, for example:

It was a long story but it was this part of the story that he liked.

a) Imagine you need to read out loud the following parts of the text. Mark the texts to help you read it. Check that your marks are suitable by reading the text out loud.

Text 1

How would you like to make the decision of going to university and being in debt for many years or getting a job?

Many English students wishing to study at university now face such a difficult decision. The opportunity of going to university was once one not to be missed. Not only did you become highly qualified, opening up top jobs but, at the same time, it was an opportunity to break away from home: to be responsible for yourself and your own finances. It was a transitional period between being dependent on parents and being independent.

Text 2

In the last twenty years there has been significant developments in government policies regarding further education. Going to university in the last ten years has frequently left students facing debts of £ 10,000 on average: money owed mainly to banks. Now universities are putting an extra burden on their students by charging fees of up to £ 2,500 per year. This additional cost means many first-year students will be faced with the prospect of leaving university with an estimated £ 20,000 debt. To put this into perspective this is less than a newly qualified teacher earns.

b) Repeat the marking exercise with a text of your own choice. Read it without marks into a tape recorder. Then with your marks. Do you notice a difference?

Exercise 3 a) Write a short presentation, about 400 words, on one of the following topics:
- protest songs
- a book or a film
- from grandparents to grandchildren: changes in society

b) Complete your presentation by producing a suitable handout about the topic, a vocabulary list and one transparency (on paper).

2 Reden

Reden unterscheiden sich von Präsentationen darin, dass nicht unbedingt Fakten vermittelt werden und dass visuelles Material selten verwendet wird. Folgende Punkte solltest du beachten:
- Erarbeite eine gute Gliederung.
- Formuliere Stichpunkte und lies deine Rede nicht ab.
- Reden sollten klar und deutlich sein.
- Die Aufmerksamkeitsspanne deiner Zuhörer ist begrenzt, vor allem bei einer Fremdsprache. Reden sollten daher nicht länger als 15–20 Minuten sein.

Redestil

- Verwende einen Wortschatz, den jeder versteht.
- Rede deutlich, mit guter Aussprache und Intonation.
- Halte deine Sätze einfach: Mache in jedem Satz eine klare, deutliche Aussage.
- Formuliere Sätze von unterschiedlicher Länge:
  Kurze Sätze betonen die Aussagen.
  Lange Sätze beschreiben, es werden zusätzliche Informationen gegeben.
- Durch Wiederholungen hebt man bestimmte Aussagen hervor.
  Beispiel: It is <u>a</u> difficult <u>problem</u>. <u>A problem</u> which won't go away. <u>A problem</u> which will stay with us for a long time.
- Auch mithilfe der Intonation kann man einzelne Stellen betonen.
  Vergleiche: We can change. – We <u>can</u> change.
- Verwende Stilmittel, die du kennst (z. B. Vergleiche, Alliteration).
- Einige Ausdrücke sind stärker, andere schwächer oder weicher. Welchen Ton möchtest du verwenden?
  Beispiel: I would like to … (soft and polite) — I want to (strong and harsh)
  We should … — We must …

Exercise 4 Emphasise the points made in the following sentences by using short sentences.

a) I was not impressed with him, he came and talked for half an hour and then he left.
For example: *I wasn't impressed. He came. He talked. Then he left.*

b) Which way is the way forward? Should we go to the left or to the right?

c) The town centre is terribly dirty. Everywhere there is litter, it suffers from vandalism and should be cleaned up.

d) Some difficult decisions need to be made which is not always that easy to do and often cause other people problems.

Exercise 5 Rewrite the following sentences using repetition to emphasise the points in brackets.

a) The world is a difficult place. (violent, hard)
For example: *The world is a difficult place. It is a violent place, a hard place.*

b) How can you work in here with the dirt? (mess, noise)

c) We must help fight poverty. (crime, hunger)

d) The train service is terrible. (awful, embarrassing)

e) Politicians from all parties should try to work together. (solve problems, reduce unemployment)

Exercise 6 Write two speeches based upon the text '*The educated poor*' (pages 80/81). Consider the different interests of both people and how they would react.

a) from a student

b) from a politician who supports the changes

Exercise 7 Write a short speech about one of the following topics:

a) It is time for one single German education system: one country, one system.

b) Let's not have a 'me society'.

Lösungen • *Key*

Zusammenfassung • *Summary*

Exercise 1

a) drove

b) terrible

c) tired

d) excellent

e) empty / noises

Exercise 2

(example answers)

a) She does not enjoy the film. She prefers the book.

b) She says she last saw him in France. He looked typically French, which she disapproves of. But she could see he was happy.

c) After a long walk in bad weather he is happy to find a small farm. But when he reaches the door his happiness turns to fear.

Exercise 3

a)

1	2	3	4	5	6
B	E	F	D	A	C

b) (an example answer)

Max, a sixteen-year-old, greatly dislikes his full name. When a friend visits, his mother calls him by it and uses his friend's full name, too. He wishes she would stop doing this. He wants his mother to behave in a normal way calling him and his friends how they like to be called. He finds her attitude embarrassing and gets very angry about it. *65 words*

Exercise 4 a) (an example answer)

Age of the five-TV family as teenagers create hi-tech dens

Once, families gathered around their television set and, as it slowly warmed up, discussed – or more often argued about – what they should watch. But those quarrels have gone the way of black and white sets. For the average British family with children over 16 now has five televisions in the house, researchers have revealed. And it is commonplace for older teenagers to have their own – along with an array of other hi-tech gadgets – in their bedroom, which they regard as their private domain.

Experts say children see television as an essential part of life, and because sets are now relatively cheap, they are increasingly being watched in lounges, bedrooms and kitchens.

'Television is like a utility to children, just like electricity is to adults,' said child psychologist Dr Brian Young. 'They are used to it in every room.'

Richard Perkes, of retail analysts Mintel, said that as more and more families invest in flatscreen sets, their old models become available for their children to have in their bedrooms. 'It's partly that they're cheap, partly the growing need to have one in every room, and the change in technology,' he added.

Another factor is central heating. Once an expensive luxury, it is now enjoyed by millions – meaning bedrooms are no longer like iceboxes and the living room is not the only place to watch television on chilly evenings.

But teenagers do enjoy communal viewing – with their friends. The researchers describe the modern teenager as highly territorial, with the bedroom serving as a 'hi-tech lounge' which is strictly off-limits to parents. Designed for socialising with friends, these rooms are full of electronic gadgets and games.

More than half (52 per cent) of the children surveyed had a television, hi-fi system, video or DVD player, games console, personal computer plus a sofa bed installed to impress their regular guests.

The countrywide survey focused on families with teenagers aged 16 and over still living at home.

b)

den:	a room in a house where a person can work or study in private
quarrel:	an argument
array:	an impressive collection of things: in this case technology
gadgets:	modern electrical equipment
essential:	necessary
communal:	shared/something done together
territorial:	defending their own area
off-limits:	an area where other people mentioned are not allowed

c) (an example answer)
When televisions were new, families watched them together. Today, British families often possess many television sets with teenagers frequently

having their own in their bedrooms, together with a large amount of other electronic equipment.
Television ownership, for young people, is never questioned. Low prices have resulted in homes having many sets. Up-grading models has resulted in the older ones being given to the children.
Previously, bedrooms were unheated, resulting in families sitting together in one room. Today, teenager bedrooms are very private and used as small personal areas full of their equipment. Their rooms are for personal entertainment and friends, and that means having a television to watch. *108 words*

Dialoge, Monologe und Gespräche • *Monologue, Dialogue and Conversation*

Note: All double inverted commas (“) can be replaced by single inverted commas (‘) in the answers.

Exercise 1

a) Jenny said, “Run as fast as you can!”
(Jenny said, “Run as fast as you can.”)

b) “It was an impossible job,” Mike replied.

c) “Where have you been?” asked Lucy quietly.

d) “My book,” Kevin shouted, “is on my desk.”

e) Mary screamed, “Run, now!”
(Mary screamed, “Run! Now!”)

f) “You want me to do that now? Now, when I’ve got no time!” Mark said angrily.

Exercise 2

a) “What can we do today?” asked Kim.
“Good question,” replied Tom. “What shall we do?”
“We could go to the cinema but I’ve seen all the films that are on,” Kim said.
Tom looked in the newspaper and then said, “What about a football match? Manchester are playing against some German team.”

b) The rain and the wind were terrible. Linda and John had not expected the weather to be so bad. They had left the harbour only half an hour ago in

sunshine. "Oh, John, when is it going to stop?" cried Linda. "It's horrible, really horrible."
"Look, Linda, we can either try to get back to the harbour or sail to that little island, over there," John replied. "But whatever we do we've got to get out of this storm."
"John, I'm scared. What if we sink?"
John spoke softly to Linda, "It's not that bad yet, Linda, but we've got to get to safety before it gets any worse."

Exercise 3 (an example answer)

appearance	background	personality and behaviour
dirty	*rich*	*aggressive*
clean	poor	unfriendly
elegant	educated	friendly
intelligent	uneducated	introvert
healthy	foreign	extrovert
ill	working class	loud
unhealthy	middle class	noisy
tough	upper class	quiet

Exercise 4 (an example answer)

character	age	appearance	background	personality and behaviour
tramp	37	– scruffy – dirty – old clothes – very poor – long hair – beard	– middle class, now poor – homeless – friendless – unemployed	– quiet – friendly – harmless
shop assistant	19	– attractive – modern – young – fashionable – clean – tidy	– working class – lives at home – lots of friends	– happy – lively – fun-loving – pleasant – nice

pop singer	26	– fashionable, expensive clothes and cars – can look scruffy or elegant – often changes appearance	– middle class, now very rich – many houses – lots of material possessions: cars, jewellery, paintings	– at work: an extrovert, fun-loving, good, successful – at home: introvert, quiet, hates fame and being seen

Exercise 5 a) (an example answer)

age: 65

appearance: clean, tidy, working class, older than he probably is

background: working class, not a lot of money, alone, not many friends

personality and behaviour: unhappy, sad, lonely, worried, concerned, harmless, quiet

b) (an example answer)

thoughts or feelings	described further
hurt	*badly hurt*
sad	awfully sad
lonely	terribly lonely
depressed	very depressed
worried	a little worried

Exercise 6 (an example answer)

"Hello, Jack. Is everything OK? You look a bit sad."
"Just thinking."
"Thinking about what? You look really sad. What's wrong?"
"Nothing, really."
"Come on, Jack. Nothing really? I think a lot actually."
"It's … it's just I don't know what to do. I live by myself – you know that – so I've got no one to talk to. No one to talk over my problems with."
"Won't I do? I know I'm not family or anything but I can listen, maybe I can even help."
"Oh, I don't know. It's sort of embarrassing – personal. You know what I mean?"

"Look, Jack. I'll get us both some tea then you tell me what's wrong, OK? There's no arguing. I hate seeing you looking so sad and miserable."
"Tea. Now what's wrong?"
"I've got a sister in London. But she's very ill. She's alone, too. She wants me to visit her but I've... I've got no money. I've never been rich but now I can't even afford to go see my own sister in hospital. Isn't that awful? My own sister and I can't afford the bus fare." *188 words*

Exercise 7 (an example answer)
As I entered the café I saw the old man sitting by himself. "Hello, Jack. Is everything OK?" I asked. It was clear everything wasn't OK but I still continued speaking. "You look a bit sad."
"Just thinking," was the answer he gave without even looking at me.
"Thinking about what?" I replied, but then I saw his face. "You look really sad. What's wrong?"
Still staring across the room he said, "Nothing, really."
I could have shouted at him. "Come on, Jack!" I replied, "Nothing really? I think a lot actually."
Suddenly, he began to talk. "It's... it's just I don't know what to do. I live by myself – you know that – so I've got no one to talk to. No one to talk over my problems with."
"Won't I do?" I asked. "I know I'm not family or anything but I can listen, maybe I can even help."
He went very quiet again when he spoke. "Oh, I don't know. It's sort of embarrassing – personal. You know what I mean?"
I couldn't leave him sitting like that so I decided to do something. "Look, Jack, I'll get us both some tea then you tell me what's wrong, OK? There's no arguing. I hate seeing you looking so sad and miserable." I went away and returned as quickly as possible. "Tea. Now what's wrong?"
He spoke like a waterfall, suddenly the words came rushing out. "I've got a sister in London. But she's very ill. She's alone, too. She wants me to visit her but I've... I've got no money. I've never been rich but now I can't even afford to go see my own sister in hospital. Isn't that awful? My own sister and I can't afford the bus fare."

Exercise 8 (example answers)

a) He stared at the stranger and whispered quietly, "What do you want?"
She laughed and said, "What do you want?"

b) I was shocked. "I can't talk anymore," I said and put the phone down.
"I can't talk anymore," I whispered. My mouth was sore and I was quickly losing my voice.

c) She stood there with her nose in the air and said, "It's dark and there's a funny smell."
He began to tell me what going into a mine was like, "It's dark and there's a funny smell."

d) I could hear noises above me and I shouted as loudly as possible, "Help, someone! Someone help!"
Jenny suddenly came up with a great title for our disco to raise money for the children in Africa. She spoke four simple words, "Help, someone! Someone help!"

Exercise 9 (an example answer)

	feelings	thoughts
me	scared, frightened, excited, worried, free	what if we crash?, it's fun, it's relaxing, hate it, don't ever want to do it again
my friend	happy little anxious concerned excited stressed	check the balloon check the weather what if he doesn't like it? have we got everything? where to land?

Exercise 10 (an example answer)

a) "Have you ever been in a balloon, Paul?"
"Never. I don't fancy it that much."
"Why ever not? It's great. You really should try it."
"Maybe some time I will. But at the moment I'm not sure I'd enjoy it."
"I tell you what. Tomorrow, do you want to come with me?"
"I don't know. Let me think about it."

"Oh, come on! There's nothing to it. It's great. You'll love it."
"I'm not sure."
"Look. I'll pick you up at eight o'clock. I've got everything. Just bring a warm hat and gloves. You're coming!"

b) "How do you feel, Paul?"
"I'm not sure, really."
"What do you mean?"
"It's fun. And you get a great view. But I don't feel that safe in the basket."
"You get used to it."
"It's noisier than I'd imagined, too. I thought it'd be quiet, no noise at all. Nothing. Just silence."
"It is."
"No, it's not. Every time you use the gas there's this loud roaring noise. The first time you did it I nearly jumped out of the basket!"
"Good job you didn't. It's a long way down."
"I've noticed that as well!"

c) "Are we losing height, Pete?"
"A little. I think the wind has changed."
"Can't we go higher? The ground's looking pretty close."
"Throw the sandbags out!"
"What?"
"Throw those bags out! Now! Quick!"
"Pete! The trees!!"
"I know. Hold on!"
"Ouch!!"
"You, OK?"
"Think so. What happened?"
"It happens sometimes. Suddenly, the wind drops and you have to land quickly."
"And this is fun? Next time leave me on the ground!"

Exercise 11 (an example is in the exercise)

Exercise 12 a) (an example answer)

b) (an example answer)
"What bull?"
"The one behind the tree."
"Can't see anything."
"Behind the tree."
"Where?"
"OK, if you want the ball, you go and get it."
"But I didn't kick it over the wall!"
"I don't care. I'm not going to get it."
"But it's my ball!"
"Well go get it then – I'll watch."
"I think I'll go get my other one."
"Have you got another one?"
"Yeah."
"Great, come on then. Let's get it. We'll get the other ball, later – when do bulls go to sleep?"

Exercise 13 (an example answer)

"What was Scotland like?"
"It was great. But there's always a mist. Especially where there's water. It's a bit scary at times."
"What do you mean?"
"Oh, nothing really. It's just that ..."
"Just what? Come on, tell me."
"No, you wouldn't believe me."
"Yes, I would."
"OK then but don't laugh. We were camping on the edge of Loch Ness."
"Oh, yes, and Nessie called to say, hello."
"See, I said you'd laugh and wouldn't believe me. Forget it!"
"No, really, I'm listening."
"OK, then. Loch Ness is in a really long, narrow valley. We were on the quiet side – camping. It started getting cold, so we lit a fire and then the mist began. You can't see anything – you just hear the water."
"Then what?"
"Nothing. Just silence and water. I got into my sleeping bag and went to sleep."
"Thought you said it was scary."
"It was. That's why I went to sleep."
"Is that it?"
"No, I woke up early and looked outside. It was still misty. Suddenly, the water became rough and small waves came to the bank. I'm sure I saw something. Something dark. Big and dark, in the water. It's stupid really. No one ever believes me – everyone just laughs. But honestly, there was something on the water and I didn't imagine the waves."
"Wow. I would have been terrified."
"I wasn't."
"You weren't?"
"No, I just wanted to see your face when I said I'd seen the monster!"

Exercise 14 (an example answer)

Suddenly the car stopped.
"What's wrong Jane?" I asked.
"I don't know," Jane replied. "It's never done this before."
"It's a great place to break down. Miles from anywhere," complained Tom from the back seat. "Anyone got a mobile?"

Everyone looked at each other. No one had a phone with them. The road was quiet and there wasn't much hope of someone driving past. I decided that someone had to make the long walk to get help.
"Looks like a long walk, then," I said thoughtfully.
"We'll all come," Jane replied.
But her friends in the back seat pointed out that it would be better to stay with the car in case help came quickly or someone drove past.
"OK, we'll all stay and Kevin goes alone," agreed Jane.
I left the car and walked what seemed like miles and miles before I saw the old house. Already I had a strange feeling in my body. I was scared. I really didn't like this place. As I got to the door, I could see it was open. I knocked and shouted out.
"Hello, is anyone there."
"Come in," an old, quiet voice answered. "What do you want?"
Not wanting to be in the house any longer than necessary I said straightaway, "Can I use your phone, please? We've broken down."
"Broken down? Everything's broken down now. Just look at my beautiful house – it's broken down, too. No one cares. They all left me."
"Sorry, I don't understand. I just need a phone. Can I use your phone, please?"
I was starting to get scared. I could feel my legs shaking and I had a cold feeling when the old man began talking again.
"It's dark outside. The roads here are quiet, you know. Accidents happen. Accidents, and no one knows why. Last year four young people broke down and no one ever saw them again."
"That's it," I said to myself, "I'm off!" I ran out of the house and back along the road. Out of breath I reached the car.
"How long do we have to wait, then?" Jane asked.
"I didn't phone anyone," I had to admit.
"What!"
"We've been sat here for two hours waiting for you! And you haven't phoned anyone!"
"Great!"
"Wonderful!"
"Now what?"
It seemed like everyone spoke at once.

Tagebuch schreiben • *Diary entries*

Exercise 1

a) (an example answer)
I do not know who is making the noise or where it is coming from but it is endless and very annoying.
The noise is terrible. It really annoys me.

b) (an example answer)
The two girls amuse me. I always watch them holding their mobiles in one hand while their fingers race over them as they send their unimportant messages to each other.
The two girls make me laugh. All they can do is text people.

Exercise 2

a) (an example answer)
Jenny never looks where she is going; she is always too busy talking. Yesterday was no exception. She was walking along the busy street, talking as usual, when she suddenly tripped over a small stone and broke her leg.
Jenny never shuts up. Yesterday she was talking so much she fell over a stone and broke her leg.

b) (an example answer)
The day turned out not to be my best one. I was cycling to my friend's when suddenly I got a puncture in my back tyre. Unfortunately, I could not repair it and had to push my bike three kilometres home.
What a day! I got a puncture. Then I couldn't repair it and had to push my bike 3 km home.

Exercise 3

a) (an example answer)
I think it is really unfair to be expected home by 11 o'clock at the weekends. My friends are all allowed out much later which means that they can go to all the discos, most of which have only just begun by the time I am supposed to be at home. *51 words*

Home by 11! Great! What fun! Everyone else is at the disco and where am I? Safely home in bed! I wouldn't mind if it was just during the week – OK, I've got school and all that – or even on Sundays. But at the weekend, that's unfair. *47 words*

b) (an example answer)
I suppose it is necessary that young people do voluntary work. We can learn a lot about others, old people for example, but on the other hand I do not want to waste my time doing something that does not interest me.
42 words

A whole year wasted. And for what? I don't get anything out of it. The only people who get anything out of it is the government. They get to save a lot of money by not giving people real jobs. *40 words*

Exercise 4 (an example answer)
... my books, the TV's terrible, my friends aren't in and now my CD has stopped working. I think I'm going to scream. Once I've decided I'm bored – like now – it's very hard to think of something to do that doesn't seem like it's only to waste time. At least 'Dear Diary' you're here to remind me of what has to be the most boring day of my life. So what is it to be? Eating, sleeping or just escaping the four walls that surround me? There's probably nothing in the fridge, it's too light to sleep, so it looks like escape. *104 words*

(an example answer)
... what there is to do does not interest me. What I need is something that is exciting, something different. I could begin the book that I always said I would write, or I could make plans to travel around the world. The possibilities are endless. But somehow even these ideas do not get me excited enough to climb out of my boredom. Perhaps boredom is necessary so that you know when you are not bored. Or perhaps life is too exciting, so that when it is 'normal' it becomes uninteresting and as a result boring. *95 words*

Exercise 5 a) (two example answers)
5th July 2004
I saw an accident today. I couldn't believe what I saw. There was a little red car going quite fast: you've guessed it – dark windows, boom boom boom, the mobile disco. I was walking along the pavement and the traffic lights were at red with a car stopped at them. Boom, boom, boom didn't stop! He drove straight into the back of the other car. Luckily no one was hurt. It gave me a shock, though. But when the driver got out, he was really angry and started shouting at the driver of the first car for braking so quickly. I think some people are blind – not to mention deaf, too!

5th July 2004
I really cannot understand the way some people drive. I witnessed an accident today that really should not have happened. A young man drove along the road with loud music coming from his car CD player and far exceeding the speed limit obviously not looking where he was going. The traffic lights at the junction had been at red for a long time and there had been a car waiting at them. Without slowing down, the young man drove into the back of the other car. The noise was terrible and it looked like someone could have been seriously hurt but luckily no one was. The young man, though, accused the other driver of stopping too quickly. I felt sorry for him, he did not do anything at all. At least I offered to be a witness for him.

b) (two example answers)
24th August 2004
Here I am feeling miserable for myself. I've just flown to Paris for two weeks holiday with my parents and what happens? On the second day, I start coughing and have a sore throat. Now, I've got a really horrible cold. I just want to stay in my room. I don't understand a word of French, so watching television is no fun. My mother came to my room earlier to see if I was OK and then left to visit the Eiffel Tower – she said the weather was too nice to stay in all day! It's all right for her, she hasn't got a cold!

24th August 2004
When you are ill and a long way from home it is very strange how lonely and horrible you feel. I've just had that experience. I only had a cold but I felt I had a terrible illness and, worse still, no one cared. That was not true, really. My parents were with me but to expect them to stay in the hotel to look after me would have been expecting too much from them. It was their holiday, as well, after all. We had come to Paris to see the sights, I could understand that they still wanted to do this. I had my mobile phone and could contact them at any time. But, it still felt very lonely not being able to speak to anyone if I needed help.

c) (two example answers)
5th December 2004
I love it! I woke up this morning and everything was white – a lovely deep white. What's really great is that the schools were closed. It's funny that in England everything comes to a halt with a bit of snow. It's automatic for kids now; snow, a dash to the radio and listen to see if the schools are

closed. I went out playing snowballs with my friends. We had a great time. It's not started again, yet – I looked out a minute ago. Hope it does, otherwise I'll have to pack my school bag for tomorrow.

5th December 2004
As usual the first snow brought chaos to the roads and the schools. England is never prepared for snow in the same way that other countries are. This morning a heavy snowfall overnight greeted everyone as they pulled back their curtains. By now we know the routine. Snow stops the school buses from taking us to school so when we see snow in the morning we turn on the radio and listen to the local radio station, they read out the names of the schools which are closed. Today, mine was on the list. It was quite nice to have an extra day at home and play in the snow with my friends. Perhaps if we have more snow during the night the schools may close again.

Exercise 6 a) (an example answer)
1st November 2004
Last night I was very cold and wet. The weather was terrible, it rained all night and I couldn't find anywhere dry to sleep. After walking for a long time I found a bridge over an old railway and made myself comfortable. Well, what's comfortable when it's cold and wet and drops of water drip from the bridge down your face and neck? It's nights like that when I wish I had never left home. But I couldn't stay there either. I don't know what my future holds. Maybe tomorrow something will change.

b) (an example answer)
5th September 2004
Yesterday we reached the summit. I couldn't believe it. I could have danced and shouted. We'd struggled up the last 100 metres. The summit was near but it was always too far away as well. Just another few metres, then another and then one more and suddenly I was there. Standing on the top of the world. I wanted to stay for hours but the weather was already turning poor. We needed to get off the top as soon as possible. In my pocket I'd brought a small teddy bear for luck. I left him there sitting like a little king looking over his kingdom. Going down was worse than coming up but after many hours we reached the tents and safety. I'd done it! I'd climbed Everest!

c) (an example answer)
23rd July 1205
My wonderful idea of a round tower to decorate the beautiful city of Pisa is slowly becoming a nightmare. Today my builders told me that people were now coming from miles away just to look at the tower that leans. I wanted them to come because of its beauty not because it is falling down before it is even finished. Forever, I will be known as the architect whose buildings lean over. What shame. How can I ever explain what has happened? I can't. Every day the tower seems to lean a few centimetres more. And every day more and more people come to see it. And every day I wish it would fall down and be forgotten about, then I could once again live without the embarrassment of being responsible for the most useless building in the whole world.

Exercise 7 a)

1	2	3	4	5	6	7	8	9
C	G	I	F	D	B	A	E	H

b) (an example answer)
Lemar's character: appears pleasant, a realist, relaxed, not boastful, dedicated, tries hard, motivated, quiet
his feelings: tries to be relaxed, gets nervous, hides emotions, holds back feelings
the situation: Fame Academy, music school, highly competitive, last show, didn't win
the outcome: didn't win, no interest in him for a long time, eventually had interest shown

c) **entry 1:** (an example answer)
Friday, 15th May 2004
It was an exciting day yesterday. I got to sing with Lionel Ritchie. Many stars helped me but Lionel was really great and gave me a lot of advice. By the time the rehearsal began I just panicked. Normally I can control my emotions but I was really nervous – I forgot the words. Lionel again was super, he talked to me and got me relaxed. Fame Academy is a strange place. All week everyone wants to help you but then, on the show, everyone starts attacking you; everyone who you trusted before and who was interested in helping you. I know it's for television and it's perhaps my

only chance for fame but it is still hard. Now, I'm relaxed for the show. Let's see what happens.

entry 2: (an example answer)
Friday night, 15th May 2004
Lionel was really great he was so relaxed and singing with him was like being with a friend. My nerves soon went away but I thought I was going to be terrible. The area where we sing is quite small with the jury on one side, cameras all around and the audience is in front of you. For one moment, though, I had a terrible thought – my family and friends are there to support me but so are everyone else's and they want me to lose. It's horrible; but the lights went on, the music began and I just did my best.

entry 3: (an example answer)
Saturday, 16th May 2004
I didn't expect to win but then again I didn't expect to lose either. Being third is OK, though. The one thing I've learnt is to believe in yourself and this I do. I want to be a singer and I know I can do it. The show gives you the chance of getting noticed. But it is so awful to stand there after you've worked so hard and be criticised. Some people get attacked for how they look, others for their voice, it is very hard to take this. You can't even reply and say, "that's unfair, I did that because…" I'm disappointed at not winning but that's how life is. There's a certain emptiness now. The show's finished, I learnt a lot, but I didn't win. What next?

entry 4: (an example answer)
Thursday, 21st May 2004
I'm getting quite worried. My performance was OK even though I didn't win but no one has contacted me yet about the show. I expected a few offers by phone or a letter, or something. Not just nothing. I haven't been out much either. I don't really want to meet people I know and I don't want to be far away from my phone. I keep telling myself that I am good but it's slowly getting harder and harder to believe anymore in myself. I haven't even sung in the last few days. I'm finding these days after the show much worse than the show itself. There, I was just nervous but it was only for a short time, then it was into action and, next, everything was over. Now I just sit, waiting, thinking, hoping. I don't know what to do.

entry 5: (an example answer)
Monday, 2nd June 2004
At last! After weeks of nothing I got two offers today. I just can't get rid of the big smile on my face. I wanted to run out into the street and shout,

"Hey, look it's me. I've got an offer!" I've been on the phone all morning to my friends and family. I was becoming so worried. Fame Academy seems so long ago, now, and I really started to think that no one was going to be interested in me. But, two offers! Maybe more will come but I must take these two. One is for an audition in a new musical. It's not really my thing but it means I can sing and, who knows, maybe something else will come from it. The other is by a really minor record company. They'll give me a short contract and see what happens. I know it isn't the great break I had hoped for but it's a start. I'm really excited.

Einen Text mit begrenzter Wortzahl schreiben • *Writing with a limited length*

Exercise 1 a)

	good	average	poor
I think cars should be banned from town centres because they cause many problems.	☐	☒	☐
Traffic-free town centres are a dream, the reality of achieving them is impossible.	☒	☐	☐
I think, in my opinion, that people with cars should be able to go to the shops in them.	☐	☐	☒
There are too many cars in most town centres and therefore they should be banned.	☐	☐	☒
Without vehicles being able to enter town centres, town centres would stop functioning.	☒	☐	☐
Town centres rely on trade. People bring that trade and vehicles bring people to town centres.	☒	☐	☐
Why should vehicles enter town centres at all? My opinion is that most don't need to.	☐	☒	☐

I think cars should be banned from town centres because they cause many problems.

The start is acceptable but the question refers to traffic and not only cars.

Traffic-free town centres are a dream, the reality of achieving them is impossible.

The sentence starts by clearly stating two points. One, that the writer supports the concept. Secondly, that an ideal solution is not possible.

I think, in my opinion, that people with cars should be able to go to the shops in them.
The repetition of 'I think' and 'in my opinion' is very poor and is unacceptable. The question does not only deal with cars, but asks about traffic. It would be better not to use 'I think' or some similar phrase in the answer since it is asking for a general opinion rather than a personal one.

There are too many cars in most town centres and therefore they should be banned.
This is very simplistic and shows that the writer has no real understanding of the theme or the different arguments that could be applied and therefore discussed. Also the question is about traffic in general not cars alone.

Without vehicles being able to enter town centres, town centres would stop functioning.
The writer starts with looking at the reality of the situation. It is clearly put.

Town centres rely on trade. People bring that trade and vehicles bring people to town centres.
A short first sentence makes a powerful start. The logical progression of ideas builds up the introduction.

Why should vehicles enter town centres? My opinion is that most don't need to.
The rhetorical question at the start gives a good beginning and a starting point to build from. The 'my opinion' weakens the initial opening. Consider how the sentence could have been much stronger and allowed the use of more words later in the answer: *Why should vehicles enter town centres? Most don't need to.*

b) (an example answer)
Some traffic is necessary in town centres, for example delivery vehicles. Buses and taxis also need to be allowed there. However, there should be parking opportunities away from the centre. In larger cities, good 'Park and Ride' systems should be available. If cars become banned from town centres, there is a danger that shops could lose business because people will go to places with parking, mainly the large out-of-town centres, which would probably see the car ban as an ideal opportunity to develop even more shops on outskirts. Eventually, people could stop using town centres altogether resulting in many shops there closing. *103 words*

Exercise 2 (an example is given in the explanation box, page 22)

Exercise 3 (an example answer)

Germany faces many problems at the moment. However, dealing with unemployment is the most important issue for the country's future.

If people work, they are happier, social problems reduce and they pay taxes instead of being paid from the state. Young people can see a future and older ones feel valued. Unemployment needs to be greatly reduced. Jobs are often available for people but not in their own areas. The government needs to encourage people to be mobile and take up these positions. It should be much easier for people to begin their own businesses, too. Employers should also be able to hire and fire when they need to.

If ignored, a generation of unemployed people will be created. The government needs to work together with all political parties to develop a way forward for the future. People's mentality to work needs to change. Mobility and flexibility are called for. *151 words*

Exercise 4 (an example answer)

Travelling today is very easy and relatively cheap. In addition there are many opportunities for young people to visit other countries, for example by short exchanges, or whole years abroad.

Visiting a foreign country is always interesting. You come into contact with the language, the food and the people. And, if there is the opportunity to stay with a family, it should be taken. In this way you can experience daily life and not just be a tourist seeing things on the surface.

Periods abroad give you new experiences. They also give you confidence. It is easy to stay at home where everything is familiar. But by going abroad you get to understand more about foreign people, their culture and their ways.

I believe that young people, whenever possible, should be encouraged to travel. It does not matter how long the period is, what is important is that the opportunity to do so is not missed. *156 words*

Exercise 5 (example answers)

a) I think CDs are too expensive. If they were cheaper, more people would buy them.
CDs are too expensive.

b) Many young people wear fashionable clothes in school.
I believe fashionable clothes in school should not be forbidden because everyone should be free to wear whatever they wish.

c) All-day schools are being discussed in Germany.
In my opinion, the problem with all-day schools is that in the afternoons children will be tired and will not learn as much.

d) Some people are worried that skiing damages the environment.
I am against skiing and believe it should be stopped because it damages the environment.

e) Many shops now put their Christmas lights and decorations outside in November.
November is far too early for shops to have their Christmas lights on and decorations outside. I think by doing this Christmas is spoilt.

Exercise 6 (an example answer)

For

It is essential for the EU to have a common language similar to a common currency. As more and more borders open up the opportunities for businesses and people to work in differing EU countries grow and a common language is therefore necessary. English is already the world language; it would be logical to make it the official language of the EU.

Against

Countries within Europe all have their own languages, they should continue to use them. The EU is a big organisation which is slowly taking away the differences between countries. The euro is an example of this and adopting English as the language of the European Union would strip away any sense of individuality which still remains. The EU should not take away people's culture.

Exercise 7 (example answers)

a) *Comment on the latest fashion trend in Britain.*
In Britain the latest fashion trend is long pointed shoes. There is concern that some people are cutting off their toes to fit into these shoes. Amputating toes is not what fashion is about. Doctors should not allow this to happen. If the pressure to wear fashionable items is so great, then perhaps there is something wrong with the fashion houses that design these items knowing most people are unable to wear them.

b) *Summarise the latest fashion trend in Britain.*
Long pointed shoes are the latest fashion in Britain. Some people, though, are amputating their toes in an effort to wear them.

c) *Express your opinion on the latest events in Britain.*
People should not be so influenced by fashion. If someone wishes to wear long pointed shoes, for example, then that is fine. I think that amputating your toes for fashion should not be allowed. I find the people who do this very sad. They are prepared to damage their bodies for shoes.

d) *Outline how fashion influences people.*
The latest fashion for long pointed shoes in Britain just illustrates how fashion influences people. The need to have these shoes is so great that people are willing to damage their feet forever by having toes cut off.

Exercise 8 a) (an example answer)
Accidents do not just happen to young people but unfortunately many do. They drive too fast, want to show off, make wrong decisions, and have little driving experience. But how can this situation be improved?
The concept of trying to reduce the number of accidents involving young people by limiting the power of a car sounds, at first, very positive. By doing this young people would gain driving experience with a car they can handle. Unfortunately, though, there are disadvantages. Low-powered cars can still go fast and any restrictions might stop people from driving completely during the three-year period because the only car they could use would be the family one, therefore not gaining any experience. And why just young people? New drivers of any age should come under the same rules.
On the surface the idea might seem a good one but it will not stop people driving fast nor will it give drivers more experience. *157 words*

b) (an example answer)
I believe that developed countries have a responsibility to third-world ones. They should not allow them to make the same mistakes. The financial cost would be high but the environmental cost would be much higher.
Developed nations have experienced the harmful phases of industrial growth. They know what that means in terms of pollution. Smoke from chimneys damaging the air that people breathe, waste products dumped in rivers, lakes and oceans. Land that is forever unusable because no one cared. Lives and nature damaged because of industry. What happens if the rainforests are allowed to be cut down, for example? Is the answer to turn and look the other way pretending nothing is happening or to stop developing countries progressing in this way? The world needs to be protected and the industrialised nations can do this. Telling poor countries not to progress in a certain way because of the harmful outcome needs to be supported with financial help.
I would like to see developed countries taking a real interest in how third-world ones grow. Large industrial groups should also help and not take advantage of poorer areas. Everyone has a responsibility to make sure that the mistakes of the past are not repeated. *207 words*

c) (an example answer)
Technology is advancing very quickly. Each step forward results in everyday objects being up-graded to include the latest technology. The time must be soon when this method is questioned. Is a future of high technology in everything we use what is wanted?
Mobiles are a good example. Some functions are useful and having a phone that can do everything from sending photographs to linking up with your home computer maybe fun or, in a very few cases, an advantage but the majority of people just need a phone to communicate with. There are other cases of over-technology, too. Most people use their computers for only a small part of what they are capable of doing. And, why should an expensive computer be outdated in a few years? Perhaps, basic models of everyday objects should be on the market, too, so that customers have a choice. Why buy a camera with thousands of applications if all you use it for is holiday photographs?
Advances in technology need to be made. However, putting the latest technology into every object that is on the market results in products being quickly outdated and over-complicated with many unnecessary and needless functions. Objects should not lose their basic use. The way for-

ward is to have a choice in what you can buy. Having no choice in the technology that you purchase is not customer friendly. Having things with multi-functions where multi-functions are not required is like always having to buy the top-of-the-range car when you just need one to travel a few kilometres every day. *259 words*

Beschreibungen • *Descriptive writing*

Exercise 1 (example answers)

a) She ran quickly towards the door.

b) The door opened suddenly but no one was there.

c) They both sat quietly together.

d) He was terribly scared but he still entered the building.

e) The young woman drove her sports car dangerously along the country roads.

f) She was very happy but terribly sad, too.

Exercise 2 a)

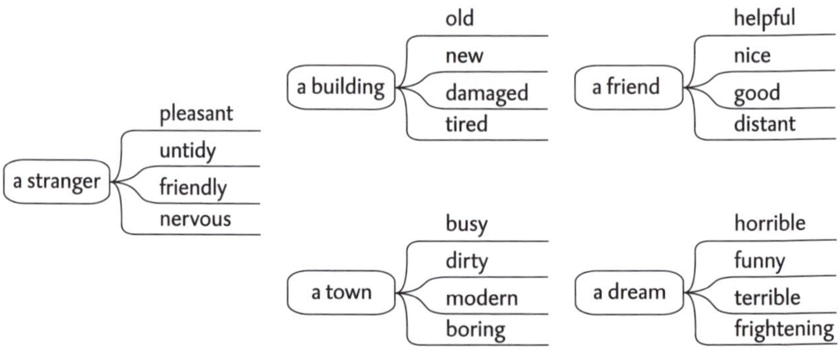

b) (an example answer)
The pleasant stranger began to speak. / The nervous stranger worried me.
The old building was no longer there. / The damaged building was being repaired.
The dirty town was unloved by everyone. / The busy town had a life of its own.
He was a very good and helpful friend. / She was a distant friend.
The horrible dream woke me up. / I had a funny dream.

Exercise 3 (an example answer)

a) **sky:** cloudy, bright, clear, calm, (morning, evening, patchy)
coast: flat, rocky, empty, unfriendly, (picturesque, remote, romantic, dangerous, rugged, hostile, hilly, mountainous)
sea: calm, smooth, blue, peaceful (inviting, dangerous)
path: narrow, twisting, thin, rough (stony, weather beaten, wet, dry)
lighthouse: white, bright, clean, rectangular (solid, small, low, squat, pretty, picturesque)

b) (an example answer)
sky: It's a calm day at the lighthouse, the sky is cloudy but it remains bright and clear.
coast: The picturesque coast is quite flat at Hogan's Point but in the distance hills rise out of the sea.
sea: The deep blue, inviting sea makes you want to swim in it but in minutes all that can change.
path: The narrow, twisting path leads to the lighthouse across the rough rocks sticking out of the sea.
lighthouse: The solid, white, rectangular building was the squat lighthouse.

c) (an example answer)
As we arrived at Hogan's Point the weather became calmer. There was still a cloudy sky but it was bright and clear. The sun shone on the white of the squat, rectangular building making it even more picturesque than normal. The coast in the distance had high cliffs but here the land was low-lying, level and the water's edge was easily got to. The sea was a deep, inviting blue but icy cold. Swimming was far too dangerous. A narrow path went between the rocks winding itself to the foot of the beautiful lighthouse.

94 words

d) (an example answer)

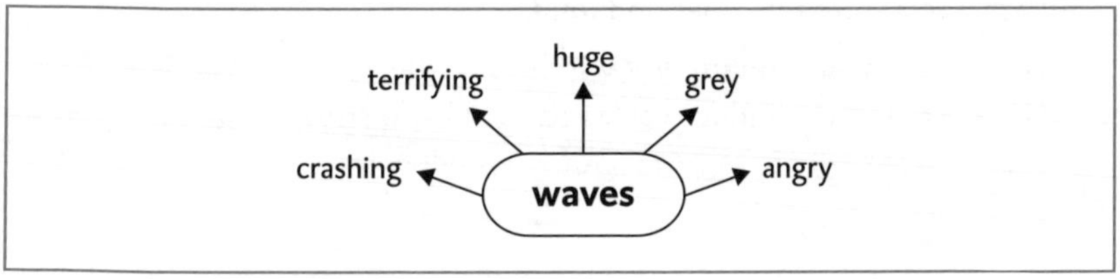

e) (an example answer)
The weather changed from beautiful sunshine to black clouds quickly coming from the west. The dark sky grew more and more threatening. Suddenly, a violent wind began and huge waves crashed against the rocks with a terrifying noise. In minutes the narrow path, which before had looked so inviting, had disappeared under a swirling mass of angry sea cutting off the low white building still bravely flashing its warning light. Nature's strength could not be stopped. The whole coast had changed its character from a friendly, gentle one to one that was dangerous and frightening. *95 words*

Exercise 4
a) The car door banged shut.
b) The waves crashed down onto the beach.
c) The old woman fought along the busy street to get to the shops.
d) The car's tyres screeched as it was driven away in a hurry.
e) There were silent footsteps in the snow.

Exercise 5 (an example answer)
a) His dirty and untidy hair was below his shoulders.
His dirty, untidy and uncombed hair was below his shoulders.
b) His face was old and wrinkled.
His face was old, wrinkled and grey.
c) It was an old and elegant building.
It was an old, elegant and friendly building.
d) The birthday party was wild and noisy.
The birthday party was wild, noisy and horrible.
e) The streets were full and busy.
The streets were full, busy and loud.
f) The top of the mountain was windy and cold
The top of the mountain was windy, cold and snowy.

Exercise 6 (an example answer)

Pieces of paper are scattered across my desk like autumn leaves on a pavement. Blown about, then left. They stare up at me wanting me to tidy them away. But I don't.

Exercise 7 (an example answer)

a) **a pencil:** The red pencil lay alone on my desk. It was just another pencil like many others. Ordinary, one could say. One end chewed, the other sharpened.

b) **a book:** The book was not very thick. In fact it was quite thin. Its cover was worn and its pages, those that were left, were turning brown; the yellow-brown colour of age.

c) **an old pair of jeans:** The jeans had been well loved. The old denim had turned into holes, patches and different shades of pale blue. They were not clothes anymore, they were a work of art, a living history.

d) **people meeting at an airport:** Smiles, happiness, joy. People shaking hands not wanting to let go, kissing, touching. Finally, with the welcoming over, the mountain of heavy bags piled dangerously high on the airport trolley begins to move.

e) **your mobile phone ringing:** At first there's a gentle ringing that slowly gets louder and louder as I start the search for it in the chaos of my school bag. It rings like an angry insect trying to escape from a tin can.

Exercise 8 a) (an example answer)

	description	observations
landscape	unfriendly	no houses
	hilly	no people
	empty	no animals
	remote	no traffic
	treeless	no birds
	lonely	grass
	rough	moor
	hard	
	beautiful	

	description	observations
road	thin	grass growing in the middle
	narrow	poor surface
	small	no places to overtake
	long	no traffic
	straight	
	old	
	unused	
	rough	
	lonely	
	empty	
weather	dry	no shelter
	cloudy	could change quickly
	bright	
	clear	
telegraph poles	straight	not many
	wooden	show there must be people
	old	where do they go?
	scattered	people have phones /electricity

b) (an example answer)
Jura is a lonely island. There are no trees or bushes just miles of wild, empty, open space. The narrow main road winding its way into the distance is very rough; grass growing in the middle, no cars in sight, or vans, or lorries, no places to overtake. Only the old, wooden telegraph poles, which faithfully follow the road, suggest life here. But where?

c) We just couldn't get the wheel off. We'd tried hitting it, kicking it, screaming at it but nothing worked. What a place to get a puncture! Beautiful, but empty. Every way we looked our eyes were met with the lonely landscape of Jura. Which way to walk? It was five lonely miles back to the last farmhouse we had seen hiding in a small valley, or we could walk the five or fifteen miles further. The five long, lonely miles, back were safer. The narrow road, grass growing in the middle, stretched out in front of us looking little more than a path. Only the old, wooden telegraph poles reminded us that there were people here. On we walked. Step after step, mile after mile, not a tree in sight, no houses, nothing. Just the beautiful emptiness of Jura. But as we walked we began to see the real Jura. Insects crawled, hopped and jumped across the road never risking their lives.

Birds flew high in the clear blue sky or low across the long grass. There were strange noises, too: animals, the wind, the sea. The emptiness never disappeared, like the road it just went on and on, never ending, never really changing. *204 words*

Briefe und E-Mails • *Letters and e-mails*

Exercise 1

a)	Dear Chris	Best wishes (Love)
b)	Dear Sir or Madam	Yours faithfully
c)	Dear Ms Jones	Yours sincerely
d)	Dear Mrs White	Yours sincerely
e)	Dear Madam	Yours faithfully
f)	Dear Mr Petty	Yours sincerely
g)	Dear Sue	Best wishes (Love)
h)	Dear Sir	Yours faithfully
i)	Dear Mrs Blair	Yours sincerely

Exercise 2

31 Appletree Lane
Norwich
PF67 2ST

6th August 2004

Computer City
19 Park Road
Bath
BR2 7FD

Dear Sir or Madam,

Yesterday, I saw your advertisement in the newspaper for …

Yours faithfully,
John Stuart

Exercise 3 (an example answer)

a) I would like to know the price of a ticket to the Rock in Park concert.
b) I would like to complain about the camera that I bought last week.
c) I would like to visit London in February and need some information about accommodation.
d) I saw your advertisement about cheap flights to Dublin and would like some further information about them.
e) Thank you for your letter dated (of) 6th October 2004.

Exercise 4

1	2	3	4	5
B	E	A	C	D

Exercise 5 a) (an example answer)

67 West Heath Road
Reading
R61 TH9

1st July 2004

The English Tourist Board
Dundee Avenue
London
W13 5WS

Dear Sir or Madam,

I am doing an English project about the Druids and Stonehenge and would like to have some information and a few photographs about them.

Do you have any brochures which give the history of Stonehenge? What I need to discover is why the circle was built, where the stones came from and how they were erected. In addition, I require two specific photographs: one that shows the whole of the stone circle and the other that shows the size of the stones in comparison to people.

I would be very pleased if you could send me any of these things and at the same time I thank you for your help. I hope that I hear from you soon.

Yours faithfully,
Anne James

b) (an example answer)

23 High Street
Salthouse
NW34 6RT

3rd August 2004

Dear Lucy,

Hi, how are you? I'm fine. Sorry I haven't written for a while but I've had lots to do for school.

Lucy, I want to do something different at Easter and wondered if you'd like to come with me? I want to go to Scotland. I've never been there and I've got a new tent for my birthday and want to use it. Mum and Dad say I can't go alone but it's OK to go with a friend. You've always said that you'd like to see Scotland. Are you still interested? I've got all the equipment and if the weather's horrible we can always stay in a youth hostel. Dad'll drive us to Oban so we don't have to pay for the train. It would be great fun. What do you think?

I'll phone on Sunday and you can let me know then.

Love,
Jane

Exercise 6 (example points)

will bring many new jobs into the area: true but some are temporary and may not be from the area, e. g. builders

ninety minutes to Stanstead: Stanstead is near, why is another airport needed? 90 minutes is not far to drive – 60 miles is less than 90 minutes away

traffic jams: people will drive to the airport here and we will have the traffic jams instead

expensive parking: the parking here will also be expensive, not everyone can use buses or taxis

little town: as you say, we are a little town – we don't need an airport

Europe: you can fly direct from Stanstead – outside of Europe will still mean going to a bigger airport

fly above us: this is what we do not want over our quiet town

affect the industrial areas: would you like to work with noisy planes flying over you all day, not to mention the pollution?

people in the west: who wants to live with the noise and pollution – you, obviously, do not live there

(an example answer)

9 Rose Cottages
Kently
ST6 78G

24th June 2004

The Editor
Cambridge Times
Isis Street
Cambridge
CA2 5LT

Dear Editor,

I would like to reply to Mr George's letter of 23rd June.

It's true that some new jobs will be created by the new airport but what about the misery it'll cause? And why is it necessary anyway? Ninety minutes away, driving very slowly, there is a perfectly good international airport. The traffic jams mentioned will definitely go away – they'll come here instead! And, although you might be able to catch a bus to the airport or arrive by taxi other people will still have to pay to park their cars. Airport car parks are never cheap.

We are a little town, not a big city. We do not need an airport. We can already fly direct to most European destinations from Stanstead. If we want to fly anywhere else we would still have to go there, anyway.

Planes flying above our heads are not something we want here. Would you want to work with the noise from the planes day in, day out, as the factory workers would have to do? Consider those poor people in the west, too. Who wants to live with the noise and the pollution? I imagine you do not live anywhere near these areas.

Jobs, yes. But not at this cost.

Yours faithfully,
Ken Marks

Exercise 7

a) side wall out of wood
b) shop window – blocked by the group
c) Afro-Caribbean man – violinist – student?
d) pillar – supporting a roof
e) large shop (Boots the Chemist)
f) man playing the double bass – student?
g) home-made advert for their CDs – 'Graffiti Classics'
h) violin case – CDs for sale – money
i) pavement – two colours
j) woman with a cello, sitting
k) two violinists, standing – students?
l) instrument cases

Exercise 8

a) There are five members of the band: two are young women and three young men. One of the men looks like he is Afro-Caribbean. They all look like they are students. In the middle of the group one of the young women is sitting to play her cello, everyone else is standing.

b) The instruments that the group use suggest that the music they are playing is classical, or possibly an adaptation of it. It's unlikely that they sing since there are no microphones and it would be difficult to sing and play these particular instruments at the same time. The CDs they are selling have the title 'Graffiti Classics'.

c) They are selling their own CDs, 'Graffiti Classics', for £ 10 each. They are doing this from a violin case which is placed in front of them. The CDs are displayed in the case with a home-made sign behind them. No doubt people are expected to place the money into the case and take a CD.

d) The group are playing outside a shop, a little to the left of the entrance. Behind them there is a large window belonging to the shop. The area they are standing on is paved but this has two distinct tones. This suggests, together with the pillar on the right, that the area is partly undercover.

e) For the musicians, it is an ideal place to perform. They are at the side of a large shop where many people will pass by. It looks as if the area is undercover, as well, which provides shelter from the weather. Where they are playing could block the entrance to the shop, which may be frustrating for shoppers and very annoying for the shop itself. One cannot, for example, look into the window of the shop.

Exercise 9 a) (an example answer)

10 Hill Lane
Richmond
RT5 6ZH

3rd March 2004

Mr Brown
Room 6
The Council Offices
The Town Hall
Cambridge
CA9 PE32

Dear Mr Brown,

I would like to apply for a music licence to perform in the town centre of Cambridge.

My group has five members in it and we would like to play outside Boots the Chemist on 6th August 2004 for two half-hour periods. In addition, I would like to know if it is acceptable to sell our CDs in the street while we are performing. Please could you tell me what the cost of the licence will be and how and where to pay for it.

I look forward to hearing from you.

Yours sincerely,
Carol Smith

b) (an example answer)

21 Oldham Road
Cambridge
CA3 5TR

9th August 2004

The Editor
Cambridge Times
Isis Street
Cambridge
CA2 5LT

Dear Editor,

Must we put up with these street musicians in Cambridge any more? On every corner there is loud music with so many people standing about watching these performers, blocking the pavements, that you can no longer get into the shops. Old people, like myself, and young families even have to walk in the streets to avoid them. At my age I can't jump out of the way of cars and buses.

Town centres are for shopping, not for open-air concerts.

Yours faithfully,
J. Jones

c) (an example answer)

34 Fern Avenue
King's Lynn
PE32 2ST

6th August 2004

Dear Jenny,

Hi, Jenny. Yesterday I was in Cambridge. Cambridge is a great place to visit. Outside of one shop there was a group of street musicians who were really good and funny, too. They didn't sing, they just played music. There were five of them, three men and two women. They looked like students – perhaps music students since they had violins, a cello and a double bass. They were selling their CDs, too, and I nearly bought one but they cost £10 and I didn't have enough money with me. I'm sure they sold a lot of CDs, though, because there were many people watching them.

I'll write again later when I have more time.

Love,
Sam

Exercise 10 (an example answer)

Holiday job - Nachricht (Rich-Text)

An...: weston@yahoo.com
Cc...:
Betreff: Holiday job

Dear Ms Weston,

I saw your advertisement in BritMag about holiday jobs in your hotel. I am 16 years old and would like to work in Britain during my summer holidays. The dates I can work are from 29th July to 1st September. I have no experience but my English is very good and I like working with people of all ages. I would be interested in having some more information about the jobs available and also if you provide staff accommodation because I live in Germany.
I look forward to hearing from you.
Kind regards,

Georg Schmidt

Exercise 11 (an example answer)

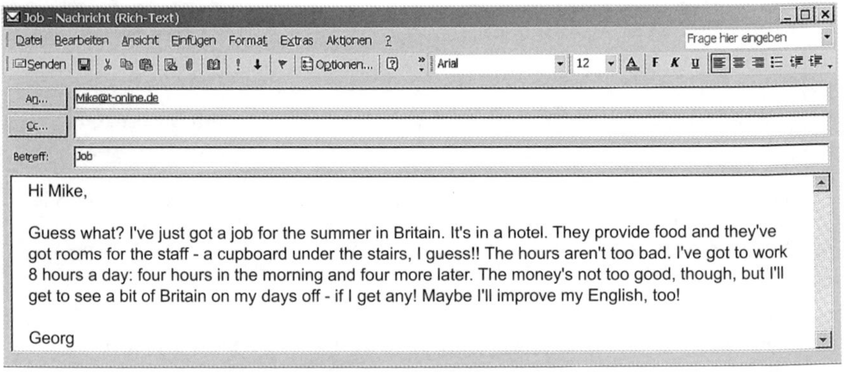

Job - Nachricht (Rich-Text)

An... Mike@t-online.de

Cc...

Betreff: Job

Hi Mike,

Guess what? I've just got a job for the summer in Britain. It's in a hotel. They provide food and they've got rooms for the staff - a cupboard under the stairs, I guess!! The hours aren't too bad. I've got to work 8 hours a day: four hours in the morning and four more later. The money's not too good, though, but I'll get to see a bit of Britain on my days off - if I get any! Maybe I'll improve my English, too!

Georg

Exercise 12 (an example answer)

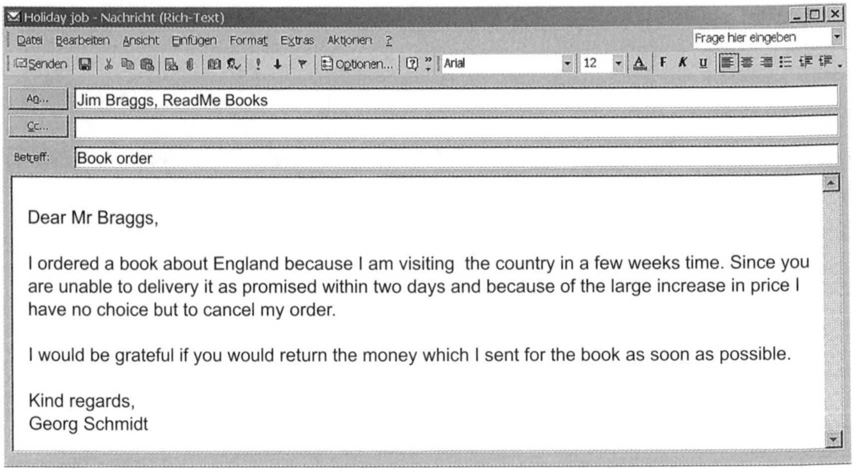

Holiday job - Nachricht (Rich-Text)

An... Jim Braggs, ReadMe Books

Cc...

Betreff: Book order

Dear Mr Braggs,

I ordered a book about England because I am visiting the country in a few weeks time. Since you are unable to delivery it as promised within two days and because of the large increase in price I have no choice but to cancel my order.

I would be grateful if you would return the money which I sent for the book as soon as possible.

Kind regards,
Georg Schmidt

Visuelle Schreibimpulse • *Visual material*

Exercise 1 (an example answer)

a) child wearing a hat – why: for protection? is he eating something?

b) young girl, Indian or Pakistani dressed in a T-shirt – is it warm?

c) figure in the background

d) a stick: why is the girl carrying a stick – is she looking for something?

e) a large cloth sack: why is the girl carrying the sack? is she collecting something?

f) the ground is full of rubbish – a rubbish dump?

g) there are shadows on the ground: it is sunny?

h) the boy is carrying a bag with handles on, he has also got a stick: why? – is he collecting something?

i) the boy is wearing a long-sleeved shirt buttoned to the neck: he looks Indian

j) both young people have a hat and something like a scarf wrapped around their heads: why? – compare this to the girl with no hat and thin clothes

k) another young person looking for something on the floor carrying a sack/bag: dressed in shirt and jacket; are these warm clothes or for protection? why?

l) other figures in the background

m) boy's sack and stick

Exercise 2 a) (an example answer)
The photograph shows four young children carrying sacks and sticks. The ground on which they are walking is full of rubbish. The children look like they are collecting things from the rubbish dump, probably waste food or objects they can use or sell. In the background there is evidence of more figures doing the same. Three of the children are wearing clothes which protect them: with long sleeves and heads covered up. Only the girl in the group is not protected in this way.

b) (an example answer)
The boy is wearing a cap with a scarf covering most of his head. He is also wearing a checked shirt, black trousers and some type of loose jacket tied in the middle. He has his head bowed as if he is looking for something on the floor. The boy appears quite young, probably not even a teenager.
In front of this boy there is another one who is also wearing poor clothing; a dark checked shirt over dark trousers. He has a cap and has some type of scarf covering most of his head. He carries a bag, or possibly a sack, in his left hand and a stick in his right hand. He looks Indian.
The young girl is dressed differently from the boys. She wears a T-shirt and nothing on her head. She is clearly Indian or Pakistani. In her hand she has a stick and a large cloth sack for collecting things. The sack appears to be about her size, the girl, therefore, is quite small and young.
Behind the girl there is another boy. Again he is dressed in a long-sleeved, checked shirt. He is wearing a wide rimmed hat, which looks like it is for sun protection. He appears to have stopped searching and is eating something. His sack is at his feet and he has his stick under his arm.

Exercise 3 (example answers)

a) The children are probably collecting food off the rubbish dump because their families are poor and they have not got enough money to eat.

b) The society in which they live must be a very poor one.

c) It is taken in a country where there is much poverty. The children are dark skinned and look either Indian or Pakistani.

d) Collecting food from the rubbish heap is work for the children. They do not have any adults with them. It is likely that the children do not go to school and, therefore, will remain uneducated. They live their lives from day to day and will probably have no real work in the future. Their families must be very poor and probably their parents do not work and the families live in poor housing. The conditions in which they live are third-world ones.

Exercise 4 (an example answer)

a) a street scene
b) outside a grocer's shop: fruit and vegetables in cardboard boxes on the pavement
c) two Asian women: one wearing a sari: an Indian?
d) an Asian man selecting fruit
e) two women in the background: both Asian and carrying shopping bags
f) a young boy on a BMX bike/small mountain bike crossing the road; again Asian
g) cars in the background
h) a typical British terraced street: an inner-city area?
i) why are there no white people? an Indian community in Britain?

Exercise 5 (an example answer)

The photograph is of a typical terraced street in Britain. The houses on both sides of the street look in good condition. There is no evidence of litter or poverty. The terraced housing, though, looks like it could be in an inner-city area. There are cars parked in the street but no moving traffic. It is a quiet residential area. There is also a young boy crossing over the road on a small mountain bike or a BMX bike. All the people in the photograph are Asian and look Indian. There are no white people. There are two women carrying shopping bags walking along the street. In the foreground is a grocer's shop which has its products in cardboard boxes laid out on the pavement. The fruit and vegetables are displayed well in this area but they take up a lot of space. On the right-hand side of the photograph there is a person bent over the fruit and vegetables selecting something and putting it into a small plastic bag. To the left and in-between the boxes, possibly the entrance to the shop, there are two Indian women who look like they are together and doing their shopping. One of the women is wearing a sari.

Exercise 6 (example answers)

a) The terraced street suggests the scene is in Britain, probably England.

b) The area is probably an inner-city one. The street is clean and tidy and is not busy. The houses also seem to be in good condition even though they are working-class ones.

c) At first, one might think that the people in the photograph are immigrants but the quality of their clothes, the pleasant residential street and the people busily going shopping suggests this is a community of British Asians. This would then explain why there are no white people to be seen.

Exercise 7 (an example answer)

The photograph shows an Indian community in Britain. One can see this from the people's appearance. There are no whites to be seen and, therefore, one can imagine that there are reasons why the two communities live apart. Maybe the Indian community group together for safety or perhaps they do not integrate with the white population. Alternatively, the white population does not easily accept non-whites. This is an established community and one which provides for its own people. It is also a well-kept area.

Although the photograph has been taken to show an Indian community in Britain it also reveals the difficulties that Britain has regarding non-whites. Britain is a multicultural society but this picture shows that the different societies do not mix well. It also shows that Britain has large Indian communities that live in the older parts of the towns and cities.

Exercise 8 (an example answer)

a) the winner's podium
b) 4 members of the USA team wearing sports kit and their medals: happy, smiling, waving, holding something – two trophies
c) American flag: above the team, in second place
d) British team in first place: dressed in white kit with medals; looking upwards at the flag unhappily
e) flag is a European one for the future with an individual country added; here, British Region
f) embedded comment spoken by a member of the British team: what does it mean?
g) Chinese team: communist suits with medals, smiling and waving in third place
h) Chinese flag
i) the situation in 2012 when London hosts the Olympic Games
j) the cartoonist

Exercise 9 (an example answer)

The cartoon is set at the Olympic Games in London in 2012. It shows the winner's podium with three teams on it in their respective positions: Britain is first, America second and the Chinese third. Above each team flies their country's flag. The Chinese and the Americans are reacting how any winner would. They are happy, smiling and waving to the crowd. The British team, though, simply look disappointedly above their heads at the European flag flying above them with the words 'British Region' written in brackets underneath it. The embedded comment voices the feelings of the British athletes: that they do not like being thought of as part of Europe, their pride, like the other teams', is with their country not with a region created by politicians.

Exercise 10 (example answers)

a) Because they have to stand under the European flag instead of the British one.

b) Because they are proud to represent their countries.

c) The Olympic Games will be in London in 2012. By this time Britain will be fully involved in Europe and Europe will have become a 'United States of Europe' with the loss of individual identities. It is showing the future for Britain.

d) The embedded texts give more information needed to understand the cartoon. The 'London 2012' is to show where the scene is and also that it is set in the future, but not too far away. The embedded text in the speech bubble shows not only the athletes' feelings towards Europe but says what most people think. The European flag with 'British Region' written on it is to demonstrate what the future will be like: that independence will be lost and individual countries will have to accept being Europe instead.

Exercise 11 (an example answer)

The cartoon is a political one regarding British people's feelings towards Europe. The cartoonist is showing how the future might look if Britain continues getting more involved in European issues. He illustrates what will eventually happen: Britain will lose its independence. The British nationality will become of secondary importance to a European identity. More involvement in Europe is what the British government wants but the people see it differently. They feel no pride in belonging to Europe. The cartoon is effective because it voices clearly what public opinion is. *97 words*

Exercise 12 (an example answer)

a) inside an alien's house on the moon
b) a family scene of mother, father, child and pet
c) the Earth and space
d) the moon
e) two aliens seated on a couch in a family situation: mother and father
f) father reading his paper
g) embedded text – European mission to the moon
h) family's pet 'dog'
i) child
j) large TV set hanging on the wall
k) embedded text: Earth News, Millwall, Faliraki Bar
l) scenes of young British people behaving badly abroad – probably in Greece: drunkenness, abuse, loud, a football hooligan,
m) caption: "Please – no Brits!!"

Exercise 13 (an example answer)

The scene is inside an alien family's home on the moon. From the large window you can see the surface of the moon with its craters, the stars in the sky and the Earth in the distance. Inside, the aliens – the mother, father and young child – are sitting around their large TV set, which is hung on the wall. The mother and father are sitting together on the couch with their son sitting nearby on a chair. Standing between them is the family pet, which resembles a dog. On the TV is a news report from Earth about British holidaymakers abroad. It shows their poor behaviour; their rudeness and their drunkenness. The father is reading his newspaper which carries the headline that Europe is going to send rockets to the moon.

Exercise 14 (an example answer)

The cartoon deals with the poor image that British holidaymakers have abroad. It combines this with the news that Europe is preparing to send a rocket into space. The reaction of the alien father is similar to that of many foreigners when they suddenly realise that they will have to deal with the unsociable behaviour of the British when they are away from their own country.

Exercise 15 (an example answer)

a) four men watching the fight
b) two men fighting on the pavement: one pulling the hat down over the head of the other
c) both men wear suits
d) large shoes
e) two more men watching, both in suits
f) a woman turns her head to see what is happening: the style of clothes looks old, 1920s perhaps
g) wall and railings
h) two more figures: a man or boy and a woman: the woman's clothes look dated
i) a building: probably a guesthouse
j) light in the window stops the painting having a dark empty space in the middle of it
k) beds 4d and 6d per night: a British sign, old money
l) a street scene

l) group of four men gather outside the doorway or entrance to the building: figures look working class – jackets, shirts and ties, others with scarves
m) two dogs walk towards the fight

Exercise 16 a)

	Yes	No
There is a house in the background.	☐	☒
The men are working class.	☒	☐
Two people are fighting.	☒	☐
It is summer.	☐	☒
The street is somewhere in America.	☐	☒
The people are all wearing expensive clothes.	☐	☒
The scene is less than fifty years ago.	☐	☒
Most people are old.	☐	☒
The cheapest room is 4d.	☒	☐
The light stops the window looking empty.	☒	☐
There are two dogs on the pavement.	☐	☒
The dogs are scared of the fighting.	☐	☒

b) (example answers)

a) (no) The building in the background is a cheap guesthouse; the prices are in the window.

b) (yes) During this time, working-class men often wore suits with cloth caps and scarves around their necks. There is nothing which shows people have money.

c) (yes) One man is pushing the other man's hat down over his head.

d) (no) Some of the men are wearing scarves and the women do not look like they have summer clothes on.

e) (no) The cost of the beds are in old British money and not dollars or cents.

f) (no) The people are wearing normal clothes for that time.

g) (no) Because of the style of clothes that are worn the scene looks older than fifty years ago

h) (no) Most people in the painting look early middle-aged.

i) (yes) In the window the prices can be read clearly.

j) (yes) Without the light there would be a large, dark, empty space in the centre of the painting.

k) (no) The dogs are not on the pavement they are in the street.

l) (no) The dogs are coming towards the fight and not running away from it.

Exercise 17 (an example answer)

The painting is a street scene with many people in it, two of whom are having a fight. The painting has not got a lot of depth in it. You see a small part of the road and the pavement both of which go across the picture. After the pavement there is a stone wall with an entrance in it in the middle. On top of the stone wall there are metal railings. Behind the wall there is a building which looks like a guesthouse; there are no hotel signs on it, only the price of beds for the night is shown in the window.

On the pavement two men in suits are having a fight. The fight, though, is not very violent. One man is pushing the hat of the other man down over his head. There are two more men standing nearby on the pavement watching and further along a woman is turning round to see what is happening.

Behind the wall there are a group of four men standing just in front of the entrance to the building. To the right of them, just entering the picture, is a woman and a young man, or possibly the teenage son of the woman. These two figures are also behind the wall.

In the street there are two dogs that look like they have walked into the centre of the picture from each side of it to see what is happening.

Exercise 18 (an example answer)

"Guess what I've just seen, Grace? I was really shocked."

"What, Annie?"

"Well, I was walking along Station Road, going home, when suddenly there was lots of shouting behind me."

"Shouting?"

"Worse than that, Grace. Two men were fighting!"

"Fighting?"

"Yes, can you imagine it? In Station Road, too. I couldn't believe what I was seeing. And do you know what really made me angry."

"What?"

"That no one - and I mean no one - tried to stop them. The men just watched. There was even another woman there with her son. Isn't it terrible?"

"That's terrible, Grace. What did you do?"

"I just couldn't watch anymore – I was so scared. I had to go straight home and make myself a nice cup of tea."

Exercise 19 (an example answer)

Yesterday, in Station Road at about 11.30 a.m. a fight broke out between two men outside Mrs Green's guesthouse. The reason for the fight is not clear but the scene was watched by many people until the police arrived. The two men were taken to the police station but no arrests took place. It is understood from one of the people who witnessed the fight that it began when one of the men started shouting at the other. The scene quickly got worse and ended up with a man's hat being badly damaged.

Exercise 20 (an example answer)

I was about to leave the guesthouse to look for a much-needed job when I heard voices. It wasn't unusual to hear people at this time of day in the street outside but unusual to hear such loud and angry ones. When I got to the door, I couldn't see at first what was happening. A small group of men were just standing there but then in front of them on the pavement I could see two other men arguing. Suddenly, one of the men got hold of the other one's hat and pulled it hard down over the ears of the man. I don't think the man was hurt, more shocked. He certainly had difficulty seeing anything. Although a fight is never nice to see it was a bit funny to watch these two.

After a short time the police arrived and took the two men away. They were still shouting at each other. I really don't know what the problem was. I guess no one will ever know. The crowd quickly disappeared. Me, too. I'd almost forgotten that I was supposed to be looking for a job that morning. So, off I went.

155 words

Exercise 21

1	2	3	4	5	6	7
D	F	E	A	G	B	C

Exercise 22 (example answers)

a) The diagram shows which environmental issues are the most important for young people between 15–21 years old.

b) The information is presented in a bar chart which gives an immediate picture of the results.

c) In the background there are many young people demonstrating and holding banners. Many of the banners have the slogan 'Stop Global Warming'. The banners are designed like the 'stop' road sign.

d) The most important environmental issue for young people is global warming.

e) Only 8 % of young people see water pollution as an important environmental issue.

Exercise 23 (an example answer)
The survey asked young people between the ages of 15–21 which environmental themes were most important to them. The results of the survey were recorded in a basic bar chart. The top issue of concern was global warming leading the second most important issue, animal welfare, by approximately 15 %. There was then a group of issues – nuclear power, exhaust emissions, burning fuels and water pollution – which all gained much the same response. GM foods were very low on the list of issues of concern but bottom was soil contamination.

Exercise 24 (an example answer)
I feel strongly about many of the issues but I am surprised that animal welfare gained so much support. Since global warming is caused by factors such as burning fuels and exhaust emissions I am, therefore, surprised that these points did not attract more importance. I think the results are influenced by the media with the poor interest in GM foods and soil contamination reflecting a lack of understanding in these areas: everyone can understand what global warming means because the topic is frequently discussed and the effects of it can be seen.
93 words

Exercise 25 a) (an example answer)
The diagram shows how much money children between the ages of 7–16 get and where they spend it. The diagram has three main sections. To the left is an illustration of a mother giving her daughter money, probably pocket money. The girl is shown thinking about all the things that she can buy with it, from CDs to chocolate bars. The second section looks at the amount of money children have. The study began in 2002 and covers the

five years to 2006. It shows in columns how the number of 7- to16-year olds is falling but the weekly amount they receive is increasing. The final section of the illustration shows where children spend their money. A list of items is provided and the percentage of children who spend their money on these items is shown. The statistics here are split between boys and girls so a comparison of spending can be seen.

		true	false
b)	There will be fewer 7- to16-year olds in the future.	☒	☐
	Since 2002, the amount of money 7- to16-year olds can spend is getting smaller.	☐	☒
	There is little difference in what boys and girls spend their money on.	☐	☒
	Girls are more likely to buy music to listen to than boys.	☒	☐
	Most young people spend their money on toys and games.	☒	☐
	Boys spend one third less on clothes than girls.	☒	☐
	Boys do not go out very much and like to save their money.	☐	☒
	Girls and boys have similar interests.	☐	☒
	Boys prefer sport to smelling nice!	☒	☐

c) (an example answer)

The number of 7- to16-year olds is falling and the money that they are receiving is increasing. This trend has been going on for the period studied which suggests that it will continue into the future, too. This means that there will be fewer young people but they will, as a group, have increasingly more money to spend.

There are noticeable differences in some areas between the spending habits of boys and girls. The main differences concern computer and video games, clothes and toys and games. There are also some surprising statistics, for example almost twice as many girls than boys purchase music to listen to.

Overall, the survey shows that young people have a large amount of money to spend. This, of course, means this group of people is very attractive to businesses: young people spend their money rather than save it. The report also shows that society must be getting richer since children are becoming increasingly wealthier.

Zeitungsartikel • *Newspaper articles*

Exercise 1 (example answers)

a) motorway madness

b) Mann's money / Harry's gift of happiness

c) factory facelift / faced for a future

d) savage storm rages / storm causes chaos

e) snake shock / snake escape

f) a stolen scream / screaming with anger

Exercise 2 (example answers)

a) Students do work hard at school. They are constantly having to write tests, do homework and prepare for lessons. Isn't that enough?

b) Why shouldn't young people have fun? They work hard and long even though people don't notice. They deserve some time to relax.

c) If people want to smoke, that is their decision. But why should people who don't smoke have to put up with those that do? After half an hour in a restaurant one's hair and clothes stink!

d) At last shops are open on Sundays. And why should people be against it? I can only see advantages in this: new jobs, families being together and a boost for the economy.

e) If people are unemployed, then they should move to where the jobs are. Jobs don't have feet, do they? It is up to people to become more mobile.

Exercise 3 (example answers)

a) Europe is going ahead with its unnecessary and expensive space rocket programme.
Europe, at last, is going ahead with its space rocket programme.

b) Cloning is not the way forward for medicine.
Cloning is the only way forward for medicine.

c) Unfortunately, the EU will get much larger.
The EU will get much larger and rightly so.

d) Sadly, young people do nothing but spend a lot of time with computers today.
It is wonderful that young people have the opportunity to spend a lot of time with computers today.

Exercise 4 (example answers)

a) Suddenly, there was chaos everywhere.
b) The strike caused many delays.
c) The car accident happened in the town centre. / The car accident happened at the corner of St. James's Street.
d) The French President was welcomed by many people on his arrival.

Exercise 5 **Rotting wreck litters beach**

It's shameful how nothing is done about the old fishing boat that has laid on the edge of the beach for numerous years now. It's time to do something about it. Who are the owners of this burnt-out wreck? Shouldn't they be told to remove this dangerous boat? For children, it looks like an ideal place to play but a dangerous one. The wood is rotten and sharp pieces of metal stick out all over. Soon there will be an accident. An accident which did not have to happen. And what about our beautiful sandy beach that attracts so many visitors? Do we want ugly wrecks to welcome them? I can hear them talking now as they leave: 'Lovely sands, shame about the wreck'. *124 words*

Exercise 6 (example answers)

a) This morning, the American President arrived in Britain to talk to the British Prime Minister.
b) After yesterday's football match at Grimsby many vehicles were damaged by hooligans returning to the station.
c) Robbie Star's concert at Wembley last night was a successful end to his world tour.
d) Demonstrators stood on the proposed motorway route yesterday holding up progress.

Exercise 7 (an example answer)

Rhino runs riot

Yesterday, a rhinoceros escaped from Woburn Safari Park shortly after breakfast and caused chaos in the area.

Robert the rhino took the opportunity to escape through a damaged area of fencing that was being repaired. Although seen as friendly and harmless the rhinoceros still weighs well over two tonnes. Robert's adventure took him across the main Woburn to Luton road causing many drivers to brake suddenly and stare in amazement. As one driver said, "Who would believe you, if you said you'd just seen a rhinoceros crossing the road?"

Robert then entered the small village of Danchester, where he quickly angered local people by eating the flowers on the village green. By the time he had got to the nearby forest, zookeepers and police had caught up with him. With fresh hay he was persuaded to enter a special cage on wheels and brought back safely to the safari park.

An investigation is now underway to find out exactly how Robert managed to escape through the fence. Local people have, for a long time, been worried about safety aspects at the park and will be talking to the management tomorrow.

Exercise 8 a) (an example answer)

News is just starting to arrive of a major disaster at sea concerning the 'unsinkable' Titanic on its maiden voyage to New York.

The luxury liner left Southampton on 10th April with over 2,200 passengers on board and by late last night was crossing the Atlantic in calm seas. We understand that shortly before midnight the ship collided with an iceberg which severely damaged it. Before help could arrive the ship had sunk with the loss of many lives. So far only about 700 people are said to have survived, mainly women and children.

The owners of the Titanic, the White Star Line Company, were unable to provide more details. They advised worried relatives to contact their Southampton office. No further comment would be made until they had been able to talk to the survivors.

b) (an example answer)

How could this disaster happen? The newest and safest ship of the White Star Line Company sank in less than three hours. 1,500 lives lost. Why?

The designer of the Titanic had provided the ship with enough lifeboats for all the passengers to have a place in one, if disaster struck. But the company, for the sake of allowing passengers an extra few metres of space on the deck, took half of them away. How could this be allowed to happen? Safety at sea should be of the highest priority. We are an island people and we all know the sea and its dangers.
Urgent safety laws need to be made. Every boat should have enough lifeboats for its passengers and crew. Crews should be trained to handle panicked people and be able to launch the boats. No boat should ever be allowed again out to sea without satisfactory safety equipment.
Let us learn from this disaster and make sure another one never occurs.

c) (an example answer)
In New York many of the survivors of the Titanic tragedy began to talk about the disaster for the first time since they landed yesterday.
Rich passengers or poor emigrants, their fates were much the same. But many had simply no chance to escape at all. A few survivors were willing to talk to reporters and give their stories of events in the Atlantic Ocean on that tragic evening a few days ago.
14th April was just another day on the ship for most passengers. Mrs French, a married woman travelling with her businessman husband, had had a wonderful evening eating and dancing into the night. As they sat talking with friends the ship's engines suddenly made a terrible noise and the whole boat shook. Mrs French was then thrown hard against the table.
In her own words Mrs French told the horror of that night. "The few passengers who were still in the lounge just looked at each other. A few minutes later the ship began to lean. Someone announced that the ship had a small problem but not to panic. But panic quickly broke out as the ship continued to lean over and people rushed to the lifeboats. The captain and his crew would only let the women and children into the boats. The men just stared. I think they knew what was going to happen. I shouted farewell to my husband and then the lifeboat dropped down to the sea. Quickly the crew rowed the boat to a safe distance and we watched in horror as the ship slowly sank. People covered their ears to stop themselves hearing the screams for help. We could do nothing."
"We just sat in the boat, no one spoke. What could we do? We were cold, wet, and frightened. After many hours another ship arrived and we were taken on board. But so few people had survived."

This tragic disaster has left a lot of unanswered questions. Why, for example, did the Titanic not slow down when it heard that icebergs were in the area? As people begin to tell their stories then perhaps what really happened on that night might become clearer and who was responsible. Already people want to know why the California did not respond to the Titanic's call for help. And what happens now to all those people whose lives have been shattered by the disaster?

d) (an example answer)
Titanic tragedy!
Safety at sea
The night of horrors

Exercise 9 ad lib.

Exercise 10

1	H	E	A	D	L	I	N	E													
2	S	U	B	-	H	E	A	D	I	N	G										
3	L	E	A	D	E	R															
4	C	A	P	T	I	O	N														
5	C	O	L	U	M	N															
6	T	A	B	L	O	I	D														
7	B	R	O	A	D	S	H	E	E	T											
8	E	D	I	T	O	R	I	A	L		C	O	M	M	F	N	T				
9	L	E	T	T	E	R	S		T	O		T	H	E		E	D	I	T	O	R

Kreatives Schreiben • *Creative writing*

Exercise 1 (an example answer)

- **the demonstration**
  - against what? unemployment
  - someone watching
  - a policeman's viewpoint
  - demonstrator's view
- **characters**
  - main character: a demonstrator: loud, noisy, angry
  - banner waving, student-type, scruffy …
  - other people: demonstrators/people watching/police
- **setting**
  - high street
  - noisy, loud, angry
  - busy, many people, police escort
- **plot**
  - demonstrator throws eggs at politician
  - arrested
  - on TV, views – government and unemployment
- **intention**
  - telling story of one demonstrator
  - describing feelings and frustrations
  - describing atmosphere
  - show how a situation develops out of control

Exercise 2 (an example answer)

a)

James	early 20s	educated, middle class	quiet, gentle, does not like angering people or hurting them but likes being with people	pleasant, clean, tidy, smart

James is one of those people who is always there but seldom says anything. He is young, in his early twenties, and well dressed. It is not that he has nothing to say, he has had a good education, but he never likes to anger people or disagree with them. He would never hurt anyone.

b)

Sue	teenager	at comprehensive school, middle class, from the city	friendly, happy, fun-loving, outgoing	modern, fashionable, typical teenager, pretty

Sue is a typical fun-loving, happy and friendly teenager. She looks modern and fashionable and comes from a middle-class family. Currently, she is still at school in the city where she lives.

c)

Tom	middle 20s, looks older	working class, unemployed, poor, football fan	aggressive, nasty, loud, tough	untidy, long hair, tattoos, earrings, fat

Although Tom is still a relatively young man, in his mid-20s, he looks much older. His appearance pleases him but he is overweight, has long hair, tattoos and wears earrings. His outward appearance is not that attractive. He is unemployed, which means he does not have anything to do and this could be the reason why he is aggressive and loud. He is a serious football fan but his looks and unpleasant behaviour often cause him problems.

d)

a shop assistant	late 50s, looks younger	working class, experienced	pleasant, caring, helpful	neat, tidy, well-dressed, greying hair, not thin nor fat

The shop assistant is in her late 50s nearing retirement. She has no great education behind her but many years of experience instead. She is pleasant, caring and helpful. She tries hard to look nice and keep herself attractive. She is well dressed and although her hair is greying she looks younger than her real age.

e)

a taxi driver	mid 40s	working class	talkative, helpful, pleasant	drives fast, fat, jeans, T-shirt, smokes

The taxi driver is very helpful and never stops talking when he has got a passenger with him. He often drives too fast but safely. He smokes too much but he will always ask his passengers if he may. There is no need for him to dress well so he prefers to wear comfortable clothes such as jeans and T-shirts. Although he is only in his mid-40s his unhealthy lifestyle is already beginning to show: he is overweight.

Exercise 3 (an example answer)

strong: Jane holds a strong point of view on everything and always wants everyone to listen to her. She takes over conversations and people quickly get tired of her. She is quite lonely and has very few friends but does not understand why. *42 words*

weak: Jeremy can never explain what he believes in. He gives the impression that he has no strong views about anything. People, therefore, often ignore him or don't ask for his opinion. He is a quiet person who prefers to be by himself. *42 words*

biased: Kim does not listen to other people's viewpoints when they are in contrast to hers. Once she has formed an opinion, nobody can alter it. She believes everything American is bad, for example, but has never been there or spoken to an American. Kim never has time for anyone. *49 words*

unbiased: Paul will listen to anyone and always tries to look at all sides of an issue. He usually has great difficulty in expressing his own opinions because he attempts to understand everyone else's. A quiet, listening and thoughtful person. *39 words*

radical: For hard decisions you need Jake. There are no grey areas with him, everything is either black or white with extremes always being supported. He has strong views and he does not allow people time to argue with him. Young, energetic and idealistic. *43 words*

conservative: Mary is typically middle class. She is not adventurous, will always support the majority and never considers anything radical or extreme. Changes only happen slowly with Mary. Friendly, pleasant and educated but not exciting in any way. *37 words*

Exercise 4 (example answers)

a)

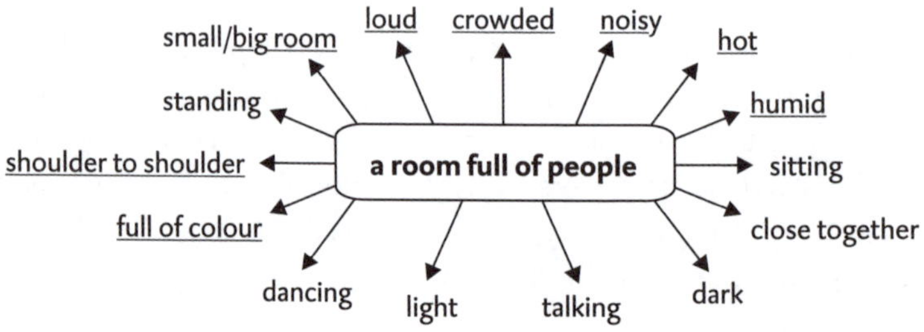

It was quite a big room but everywhere you looked there were people in it. It was loud and noisy, hot and humid. People were standing shoulder to shoulder, no room to turn or even to make a little space for oneself. Individuals became a crowd and the crowd, if you looked down on it, was a moving carpet of colour. *60 words*

b)

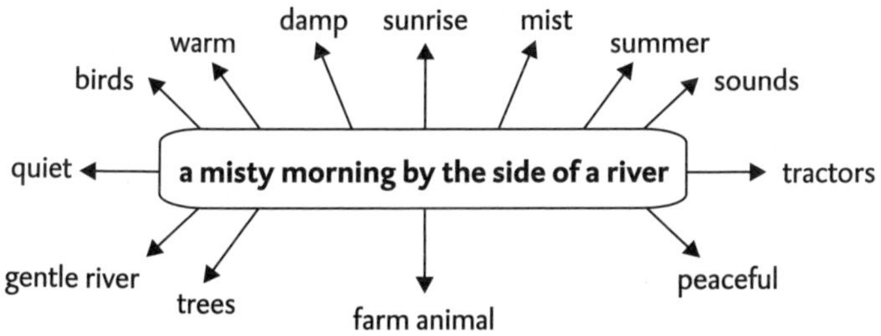

The mist lay low over the damp fields and hung on the bank of the gently flowing river. The early summer warmth was building up slowly as the sun rose above the trees spreading golden light over the riverside. The peace and quiet broken only by birds singing and the distant sounds of country life; tractors jumping into action and cows waiting to be milked.

65 words

c)

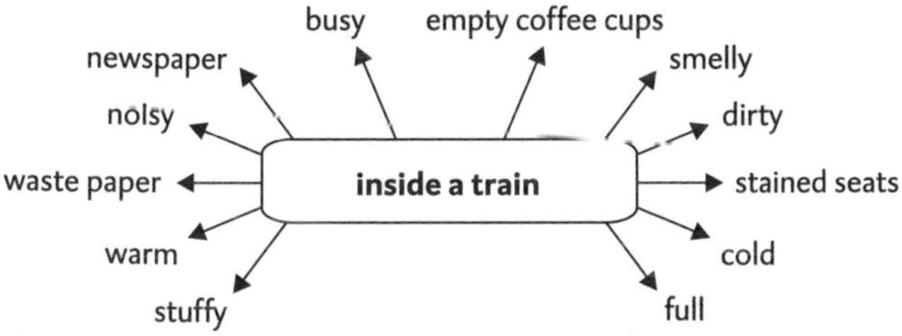

Stepping inside the train was like stepping into a different world. First the smell; stale tobacco smoke mixed with the aroma of cheap coffee. Then the attack on the eyes; newspapers on seats, waste paper left on the floor, half-eaten sandwiches, banana skins and orange peel left stinking on tables. Waste paper bins overflowing encouraging people to ignore them. The airless, overfull train departed with its unhappy passengers staring out of the unwashed windows. *74 words*

d)

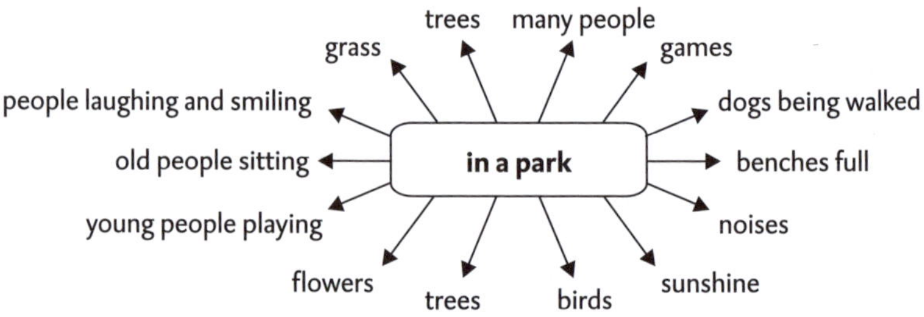

The park was full of old trees, flower beds and wide open spaces of grass. All around there were the sounds of people relaxing and enjoying themselves. People were laughing and smiling as they played games in the open air. Dogs were being walked by their owners and every bench was full: students reading books and old women watching the world pass by in front of them. *67 words*

Exercise 5 (an example answer)

(slowly setting the scene) Snow was not really expected at all so early into the winter. Normally it arrived in January or even February but this year it began on 6th December. The day started much the same as any other at that time of year, a little grey, but by lunchtime the temperature was falling rapidly. Then it started to snow. Steadily at first but after a few hours large, thick snowflakes were falling and chaos began. *74 words*

(descriptively) It was mid-afternoon on a cold and grey December's day when the winter arrived with all its strength. Snowflakes steadily fell making everything look like a charity Christmas card. Soon parked cars had become little more than white hills in a white landscape and the whole world looked like it had silently stopped. People stared out of their warm office windows glad to be inside but wishing too that they could be at home. Warnings of chaos were just beginning on the radio. *84 words*

(dramatically) Chaos. Absolute chaos. The first snow of winter and the whole world stops. The winter arrived in strength. A cold wind blew, the temperature dropped suddenly and a heavy snowfall was the result. In minutes roads were blocked and railways and buses had stopped working. People were having to walk home from work. *53 words*

Exercise 6 (example answers)

a) The mobile phone fell onto the stony path with a soft crunching sound. It was a noise you couldn't ignore. But the woman in the long black coat did just that. She ignored it and walked on as if nothing had happened. Without looking back even for one second, she quickly reached the tall Victorian park gates where a large, light coloured car was waiting. A door opened and she disappeared behind darkened windows.
Shortly afterwards a distant figure appeared along the same path. As he got closer to the phone it began to ring its melodic tone. He paused, looked about and then bent down quickly to pick it up. In seconds, the stranger had the phone at his ear and was already talking. The words that were spoken were clearly angry ones. The phone call over, the man put the phone into his inside pocket and walked back in the direction he'd come from.

b) So, this was the view that the prisoners had. It must have been terrible in the cells of the old castle hundreds of years ago, dark, damp and smelly. An underground world without light.
The room was no more than two metres long and two metres wide, just enough space to lie down on the stone floor. There wasn't a bed, just straw in the corner. There wasn't even a window, not even a high one. The only source of light was through the keyhole. As I entered the small cell and the door shut behind me, a fear unlike anything I had ever experienced before went through my body. Although the castle guide was closing the door, not a fearsome guard, I felt alone and trapped almost straightaway. There was just darkness.
After a few minutes I was really very scared, I turned around and found the large keyhole that the guide had told us about. It invited you to look out of it. I placed my eye close to the cold metal of the lock to see what I could see. Nothing! A stone wall and a corridor. But the light attracted me and I could understand how the prisoners must have spent many miserable hours just looking out through their keyholes instead of sitting in the dark of their cells.

c) It could have been a newspaper with arms, legs and wearing a dark hat but it was actually Mr Jones. He always liked to take his paper with him to the dirty, noisy factory where he worked and read it at lunchtime. Mr Jones hated the factory and had only taken the work because he needed a job. At midday he always had to escape the surroundings which he found so terrible.

Seaham Valley Park was nothing very special but at least it had fresh air, a view of the town and was quiet; it would do. When the factory siren went off, Mr Jones stopped what he was doing, grabbed his sandwiches and the daily paper that he had bought on his way to work and off he walked down the street wearing his old black hat. He usually sat on the first park bench next to the large oak tree, if no one else was there. At two o'clock he would carefully fold his paper, get up and walk to the waste-paper bin just before the exit where he would leave his newspaper. Then, for Mr Jones another boring afternoon would begin.

Exercise 7 (example answers)

a) The builders were digging deep into the overgrown land of the old factory on the corner of Viking Way. For the fifth time that day Dudley had to stop his digger.
"Hi, Mick! Come here, will you!" he shouted.
"Not again," came the reply. "I'm fed up of pulling out old bits of metal from your hole. Try getting out of that digger of yours for a change!" Mick answered.
"I'll do it myself then – what's wrong with you today, anyway?" shouted Dudley as he leapt off the machine and went across the thick muddy mess that would soon become a garage.
"Don't know why I bother," he said as he jumped into the trench he had been digging. "I could just as well leave the metal here but the boss wants it all out."
As he bent down to pull on the long piece of iron, he turned and saw something bright and shiny next to him.
"How does silver paper find its way down here – two metres deep?"
But when he pulled again at the long, thin piece of metal he slipped and his arm scraped along the 'silver paper'. "Agh!!!," he shouted but he soon stopped when the thing he'd just cut his arm on dropped at his feet.
"Now, what's this doing here?" he asked himself.

b) The bottle stood on the table, the message still inside it. Karen had been on the beach that morning, the wind was super blowing metre-high waves onto the sands. She'd seen the bottle already some distance out at sea and it excited her. Bottles, secret messages – that's what good books are made of. She couldn't jump into the stormy water, it was far too dangerous and

she knew it. So she stood there walking up and down the beach a few paces as the bottle changed course.
"Come on bottle," she whispered, "Come on."
The fourth wave is always the highest and sure enough it threw the little clear glass bottle less than a metre away from the feet of Karen. Before it disappeared back again into the sea, Karen ran onto the wet sand and got hold of the bottle just as another wave was almost upon her.
"Got you at last," she shouted, not noticing that it had cost her a wet left foot.
She didn't want to open it immediately. So she returned home and put it down on the small table usually used to stand a large plant pot on and studied the rolled-up piece of paper inside it.
"So what do you have to say, little bottle?" she said quietly to herself. "Who's the message from?"
"Why don't you open it and see!" came a loud booming voice which made Karen jump a metre into the air.
"Tim!" Karen said, shocked. "I thought…, I thought you were the bottle speaking."
"Don't be silly, bottles don't talk. Well, are you going to open it or not?"

c) The books weren't that old but their brown pages already nearly matched the dark brown covers which were torn and dirty with use. John had discovered them a few weeks ago at a car boot sale in the town centre. But since then they had just sat on his desk at home. Beth was slowly getting annoyed with John not only for buying them but for just leaving them out.
"John, can't you move these books? They've been here for weeks now. I can't even use the desk – and they smell! Where on earth did you get them from?"
"In the car boot sale, Beth. They were just lying about on the floor."
"But why did you buy them? Who wants to read 'A Seaman's …'? It's so damaged I can hardly read the title: 'A Seaman's Journey'?"
"I do," replied John.
John picked up the dusty, dirty book that laid on the top and asked Beth to look carefully at it. She still couldn't see what was so special about the smelly old book in front of her. Then John opened the book carefully and pointed to the writing on the first page. It wasn't a book after all, it was a diary. But Beth still wasn't impressed.
"Look, Beth. Look at the name."
"A Seaman's Journey by J. M. Blanche. So?"

"J. M. Blanche was my great-great-grandfather's brother. He went to sea as a young boy and that's all the family knows about him."
"Until now," said Beth.
"Exactly," said John. "Now do you understand?"
"About that book, yes," Beth answered. "But what about the rest?"

Exercise 8 When Anne got to the door of her office, Ryan's message was sitting outside it in a bottle. Anne always found this funny. Most people just put a note on the door for her but not Ryan. He always rolled it tightly up and then carefully dropped it into the little glass bottle. Some days later he'd come around and ask her for the bottle back! Anne asked him one day why he didn't leave a note on her door like everyone else – he just said it was more fun this way and at least she knew it was from him!
Anne picked up the little bottle, found her keys and opened the office door. She'd hardly had time to put down the large cardboard box she had been carrying and Ryan's message before her mobile phone began to play its Beethoven melody.
"Oh, not now," she groaned. "Don't I ever get a rest?"
She fought with the contents of her handbag until she found her mobile which, by now, was well into Beethoven's ninth. Her fingers got hold of the small black, leather case, opened it and took out the phone.
"Hi."
"Hi, Anne. It's Ryan."
"What do you want, Ryan? I've just got here. I haven't even had chance to read your message yet."
Ryan's answer surprised her, "Anne, it's the mask. It's been stolen. I came into the museum this morning and it had gone."
"Are you sure, Ryan?" Anne replied, shocked that the theft had been discovered so soon. "Maybe someone's moved it. Look, Ryan, don't do anything yet. I'll be over in half an hour. We'll search the museum and if we can't find it, we'll phone the police."
Anne threw the phone back into her bag. "Now, what?" she shouted to herself. "Do I keep it or take it back?" She moved over to the cardboard box and opened it slowly. The beautiful golden face smiled up at her.

Exercise 9 a) (an example answer)

The charge of the Light Brigade	the atmosphere before a soldier's feelings watching and realising a mistake has happened family and friend's reactions afterwards a newspaper article: praise or critical a survivor's story a Russian's viewpoint <u>a wife's story</u>
a wife's story	saw news in the street: newspaper headline sadness scared waiting for news uncertainty thinks about and remembers her husband

b) 28th October, news of a terrible battle was just beginning to arrive back in England. I remember standing in the main street on that day as if I was stuck to the pavement. All I could see was the newspaper headline tied to a piece of cardboard standing against the newspaper boy's bag. Crimea Catastrophe: hundreds killed.

I thought of Arthur. How good he had looked in his uniform. How proud he had been to serve his country. A soldier. No, not a soldier – I was told off for saying that – a cavalryman: a cavalryman of the Light Brigade.

But this news. I was so scared and worried. What had happened? Please, not to my Arthur. I grabbed my shopping, bought a paper and rushed home. I opened the door threw my bags down, my coat falling onto the floor and I stumbled into the dining room. Terrified, I opened the paper. 500 killed.

Five hundred killed but no names. The days went slowly by after that. Not knowing was terrible. Every day more information appeared. How the cavalry had made a terrible mistake but how they fought well. Heroes, they were called. But dead heroes don't return. It was some days later that I finally received a letter. That little brown envelope brought a chill to my stomach. I couldn't open it. I desperately needed to know what was inside it but my body just turned to stone. I held it in my hands for many minutes before opening it.

The only words I read were "safe – home in six weeks". *263 words*

Exercise 10 (example answers)

a) **atmosphere:** dark, smoky, busy, warm, friendly, secretive, smells
café: old, working-class, basic, busy, full, mugs, no tablecloth, curtains at the window
people: workers, talking, quiet conversations, faceless figures, one with a hat perhaps a seaman? long hair, working clothes, not old or young – ageless

b) The café was close to the small harbour, just minutes away from the main street. Everyone knew Carol's. Low ceilings, brown walls, old wooden tables and chairs: a scene unchanged for a hundred years or more. A dark, smoky place where people met and talked. Strangers were unusual there. But on this particular day a new face appeared and sat with the captain.
Not everyone liked the captain but everyone liked the fast boat that he had. But that day it was the stranger who sat with him that people were talking about.
"Who's that?" you could hear being whispered around the smoke-filled room.
"Not from around here, that's for certain."
"Saw him the other day."
"Where?"
"Looking at the captain's boat."
"Hey, Carol! Come here a minute." Then in low whispers, voices asked, "Who's that with the captain?"
Suddenly, the stranger threw back his chair, jumped to his feet and left banging the door angrily behind him. The whole café was quiet. No one spoke. Slowly the captain got to his feet, paid and left without saying anything.
"What was all that about?" asked Jim who was sitting a few tables away near the big, roaring open fire.
No one answered. But they could all guess. The captain had just said 'no' to someone who had wanted him and his fast boat very urgently. *225 words*

Exercise 11 (an example answer)

a)

a twenty-pound note is lying on the pavement

- who finds it? a tramp, his feelings?
- who lost it – rich/poor person, their reaction?
- when and where is the loss discovered?
- where is the money found? – a different country, a lonely street, a poor area, a rich area, town centre
- the note is an old one with Queen Victoria's face on it – strange, why?
- you read the next day about a robbery
- fantasy: the note has a life of its own. You try to pick it up but it moves/a dream with strange things happening

Henry slowly began to wake up. His bed was the corner of an old disused bus shelter just around the corner from Toddington's main street. He stood up, stretched his cold and aching body and began his daily routine of packing his belongings into two plastic bags and getting out his little tin whistle. He usually walked up to the market place, found a comfortable place to sit and played a few tunes badly. Once he had earned enough money he would buy a roll and something warm to drink for his breakfast. Carrying his home, Henry walked towards the High Street. He didn't like people that much. They scared him. So he walked looking down at the pavement investigating the empty cigarette packets and other rubbish with his worn-out shoes as he went. After years of living on the streets Henry's eyes were well trained to finding things that he could use. As he turned into the main street he was attracted to a folded piece of paper lying against the wall of the post office. He moved nearer, put his plastic bags down and bent stiffly to pick it up. Money a twenty-pound note. This was enough to provide Henry with a week of breakfasts, but of course it wouldn't.

Henry began to wake up slowly in his old wooden bus shelter. Around him lay the empty bottles of yesterday. Hunger was already upon him. He began to pack his bags for just another day on the streets. *252 words* b)

on the radio was her song

- which song?
- memory of someone
- on the car radio
- tears in eyes
- she wrote the song
- a song she really liked

Jenny had just said farewell to her friend Daniel. She'd met Daniel during the summer in Scotland. She had a holiday job working in a fast-food restaurant producing something and chips for the masses of tourists who came to the picturesque holiday town. Daniel came from Germany, his family owned a small hotel somewhere in the south. He was in Oban working in the same place – a working holiday before going back to university.

But the long summer days soon came to an end. Too soon for Jenny. Daniel had to return to Germany and she was going to start her studies in September. As she drove Daniel to the airport they talked to each other all the time. When an embarrassing silence began it was quickly ended by promises to write and visit and phone. Promises meant, but ones that both new would never happen. Every minute was special as the miles went by.

Promises, farewells and more promises were made at the check-in. Final waves were exchanged as Daniel disappeared through passport control.

Jenny waited to watch the plane take off. With an empty feeling inside she climbed into her car and drove out of the multi-storey car park and onto the motorway. Feeling lonely and sad she put the radio on. Tears fell down her face as she listened to a song *Daniel is leaving tonight on a plane* ... Her song.

237 words

c)

the forest path

- a walk
- an accident
- an unhappy experience
- meeting people
- jogging
- lonely
- something that scares – sounds/voices

The quick way was through the forest. Greg knew he had to be back home before dark. His parents worried about him on his bike especially as he had to ride along the busy main road. This evening Greg was late, he had for-

gotten his lights and it was getting too dark to be safe on the road. There was no choice. Greg had to cycle through the forest.
Greg hated the forest. Ever since he and a friend had had to walk through one when they got lost on a camping holiday. That day it began to rain and then thunder. Greg had been terrified.
The forest path was the only choice. A mile of track, no people, darkness creeping up all around him. Breathing heavily Greg set off, pedalling hard to get through it as fast as possible. The silence worried him. Scared him. He didn't look back. When he heard noises, he didn't look at where they came from. Every noise made him pedal faster. Now, going as fast as he possibly could, he saw the end of the darkness and a few houses in the distance. Suddenly, a wolf stood in front of him!
"Here, Rex! Come here you stupid dog!" a voice shouted.
"A dog!" Greg said loudly, sweat running down his face.
By this time the owner had Rex under control. "Sorry, did he give you a fright?" the woman enquired.
"No. No, not at all," Greg answered as he quickly rode away, his heart still racing with fear.

255 words

d)

a game
- the player
- chess, football …?
- people watching
- atmosphere; tension, excitement
- where? a special place?

The battlefield was being prepared. At the side of it, two armies were packed together surrounded by wood. Waiting, the tension building. Who would win? How many men would fall today?
The order was given and the armies lined up facing each other. The white king staring across the checked field at the opponent who dared to threaten him today.
At the sound of a bell, a horse jumped forward and looked sideways. The black king studied what was happening for a few seconds and instructed his men to be careful and sent a lone soldier out to investigate. Another horse appeared and soon both kings had their forces in action. Many fell and were taken away. Thirty minutes had passed now and the troops were looking thin on the battlefield. The white king had lost his advantage. He was being forced into a corner. Surrounded and trapped, there was no longer any hope. He couldn't win, the day was lost.

Without warning, the white king suddenly fell to the ground. The end had come. The game lost and won. The armies were put back into their wooden box, black and white separated by a thin divide ready to fight again tomorrow. *202 words*

Exercise 12 (example answers)

a) Once inside the house the woman sat down and relaxed after her busy day in the office.

b) The heavy bags which she carried made her walk slowly.

c) He looked down on the small boats in the harbour below. He never liked heights. Flying made him scared and 6,000 metres always made him feel ill.

Exercise 13 (example answers)

a) The young girl walked slowly to the bus stop.

b) It was a beautifully sunny day. She got on her red mountain bike and rode it carefully down the quiet tree-lined street.

c) There was a loud knock at the front door. Tony slowly got up from his chair and went and opened it. He looked around but there was no one there.

Exercise 14

a) She was a <u>sensitive</u> child, always crying when things went wrong.

b) <u>Recently</u> the house had been broken into many times.

c) <u>Up to date</u> / <u>The latest</u> information about the robbery is difficult to get at the moment.

Exercise 15 (example answers)

a) "Look at that house, David."
"Where?"
"In the valley, over there."
"I can see it, now. It's beautiful, isn't it? What a super garden."

b) "What was that?" Tony said suddenly.
"I don't know," Lucy answered. "Nothing to be scared about. Perhaps the wind."
Not believing Lucy's explanation, Tony replied, "I've never heard wind make that noise. I'm sure it was breaking glass or something ..."

Exercise 16 (example answers)

a) Silent footsteps cannot be heard.
Her footsteps were silent in the snow.

b) There is a storm and it is in the middle of the night, therefore *dark* is not necessary.
The storm was terrible. It was now the middle of the night. The wind blew and the rain could be heard loudly against the windows.

c) The cat does not fit the image of a ghost. It would be better to be white. A cat seldom lands noisily and noisily on soft grass is extremely unlikely. The two images do not correspond.
Like a ghost, the white cat suddenly appeared on the high wall and then sprang landing quietly on the soft grass below.

Präsentationen und Reden • *Presentations and speeches*

Exercise 1 a) (an example answer)

Vocabulary

vocabulary	usage	alternative
debt	*(to be) in debt*	*to owe money*
(to) face	face a decision	have to deal with
expectation	one's expectations	hopes and wishes for the future
significant	significant developments	important
regarding	regarding further education	concerning/about
burden	extra burden on	difficult and worrying problem
prospect	the prospect of	probability/possibility/ future chance
trend	the current trend	way things are developing

consequences for	have consequences for	an effect on
education's sake	education for education's sake	(to study for) that reason alone

b) (ad lib.)

c) (an example answer)

The educated poor

Facts

- English students face a choice: university and getting into debt or getting a job.
- During the last 10 years students have left their universities with an average debt of £ 10,000.
- Universities are now proposing charging fees of £ 2,500 per year.
- A student starting university today will probably leave with a debt of £ 20,000.
- £ 20,000 is less than a newly qualified teacher earns.

Consequences

- Many students are deciding to go to local universities to reduce costs.
- Many young people will remain dependent on parents and not have the opportunity of gaining independence and becoming responsible for themselves.
- Some young people who could go to university do not take up places because of the fear of debt.
- The question arises whether or not universities should only offer courses that are directly linked to careers.
- There is a question about whether learning for the sake of learning is acceptable.

d) (an example answer)

The educated poor

- university and debts <u>or</u> working
- universities = higher academic qualifications, prospect of better jobs, independence, large debt
- university education has become increasingly expensive
- most students will leave owing £ 20,000
- many students will remain at home
- universities might need to reduce courses
- the numbers on some courses will reduce

Exercise 2 a) (an example answer)

Text 1

How would you like to make the decision of going to university and being in debt for many years / or getting a job? // Many English students wishing to study at university / now face such a difficult decision. // The opportunity of going to university was once one not to be missed. // Not only did you become highly qualified,/ opening up top jobs / but, / at the same time, / it was an opportunity to break away from home: / to be responsible for yourself and your own finances. // It was a transitional period between being dependent on parents and being independent.

Text 2

In the last twenty years / there has been significant developments in government policies / regarding further education. // Going to university in the last ten years has frequently left students facing debts of £ 10,000 on average: / money owed mainly to banks. // Now universities are putting an extra burden on their students by charging fees of up to £ 2,500 per year. // This additional cost means many first-year students will be faced with the prospect of leaving university with an estimated £ 20,000 debt. // To put this into perspective this is less than a newly qualified teacher earns.

b) ad lib.

Exercise 3 a) (an example answer)

From grandparents to grandchildren: changes in society

A generation difference is accepted as being 30 years. So what was life like 60 years ago? Born during or shortly after the Second World War many grandparents were brought up in difficult times. A lack of things would have been noticeable in many homes: no television, no car, perhaps no fridge or freezer. But what were the positive aspects of former times? Children could play outside in safety, crime was rare, jobs were more or less guaranteed and secure.

The post-war generations witnessed a change in society with unwritten rules that became more and more relaxed. The sixties in particular saw people having more freedom of expression and showing their frustration

with old-fashioned attitudes. And as the post-war economy boomed, standards of living rose. Expectations became higher and what were once one generation's luxuries now became the next generation's essentials. No one today would question the need to own a car or the right to have a television set in the corner of the living room or a computer in the house.
As technology and know-how develop, society has experienced a rapidly shrinking world where the pace of life has subsequently accelerated.
Grandmothers probably washed by hand with one day in the week set aside for it, then people acquired washing machines to do the work. This did not allow them to sit down, read a book and be idle instead it allowed them to be able to do something else: to do two or more things simultaneously. And what once took many days can now take only a few minutes – communications, for example. People wrote letters, posted them and eventually received a reply perhaps a week later. Now we e-mail people and expect a reply the same day. And with mobile phones, everyone is accessible at anytime.
But what else has happened? The security of jobs has disappeared, the health system is crumbling, the social security system is failing, the pension system is in a crisis, unemployment is reaching record figures daily and the economy is struggling. While at home: children no longer play together like they did, preferring their computer worlds to social interaction. Streets are no longer safe areas where one could play football or tennis. As children, grandparents could run around with friends for hours without parents really knowing where they were, this would now no longer happen. And if it did, parents would be seen as irresponsible.
A changing world, but changing for the better? *404 words*

b) (an example answer)

vocabulary	usage	alternative
witnessed	witnessed a change	saw
boomed	economy boomed	rapidly increased
accelerated	subsequently accelerated	become faster
(to be) idle	and be idle	to do nothing
(to be) accessible	is accessible at anytime	available
irresponsible	be seen as irresponsible	not caring

Handout

From grandparents to grandchildren: changes in society

- A generation is seen as being 30 years. Grandparents would be born approximately 60 years ago.

Grandparents' lives

- Most were brought up in the early post-war years.
- At this time there was a lack of consumer goods.
- Life was relatively uncomplicated: children had freedom, crime was rare and jobs were secure.

The changes

- The 60s brought about social change.
- Rules became relaxed and attitudes changed.
- The economy boomed resulting in a rapidly increasing standard of living.
- Each generation saw their parents' luxuries to be their essentials, therefore expectations rose.

Today

- Technology allows us to do many things at the same time, which has accelerated the pace of life.
- Technology has also enabled everyone and everywhere to be easily accessible.
- The benefits of technology have been great but problems are arising regarding people.
- Most areas of society are facing financial crises, the economy is struggling and unemployment is continually rising making futures uncertain.
- Children have restricted freedom because of the dangers of playing outside or being alone.
- Computers are turning children away from social interaction and into isolated individuals.

Transparency

From grandparents to grandchildren: changes in society

- 30 years separate one generation

Grandparents

- had fewer things
- uncomplicated lives
- children had freedom
- little crime
- secure jobs

Changes
- 1960s
- rules, attitudes relaxed
- economic boom: standard of living rose
- expectations rose

Today
- influence of technology
- life is faster, the world smaller
- social problems arising
- financial crises, unemployment, struggling economy
- uncertain futures
- restricted freedom for children
- computers affect social interaction

Exercise 4 (example answers)

a) I wasn't impressed. He came. He talked. Then he left.

b) Which way forward? Left or right?

c) The town is terribly dirty. There's litter and vandalism. And it should be cleaned up!

d) Difficult decisions need to be made. It's not easy. They could cause problems.

Exercise 5 (example answers)

a) The world is a difficult place. It is a violent place, a hard place.

b) How can you work in here with the dirt? With the mess and with the noise?

c) We must help fight poverty. Fight crime and fight hunger.

d) The train service is terrible. It's awful. It's embarrassing.

e) Politicians from all parties should try to work together: to solve problems, to reduce unemployment.

Exercise 6 (example answers)

a) I want to go to university. I've got good A levels and I want to study. But I find the decision to go along this route increasingly difficult. If I go to university, I will face being in debt for many years to come. If I don't go to university, I will be taking a job for the money and not one I really want to do.
Even if I go to university, am I not simply being an additional burden to my family? I would like to be away from home, being responsible for myself but it looks increasingly likely that I will have to stay at home and go to the nearest university. 'So what,' people might say. The point is that university allows young people to be themselves, to break with homes and be independent.
But the main problem is money. How can anyone carry the weight of knowing they will leave university owing more money than they will earn? Is this not a great risk to take? How can students be responsible people when the government makes them into debtors? And debtors who cannot repay for many years.
And what about the consequences? Have they really been taken into consideration? Will courses be reduced? Will universities be obliged only to have courses that lead directly to employment? Will people be driven away from studying altogether?
Do I go to university or not? It's a very difficult decision to make.

b) The days of things being free are long gone. Universities need to be independent institutions, just like any business. Their product is education. If they want to stay in business, then they must become cost-effective and if this leads to fees needing to be charged, then that is acceptable. One cannot go on forever supporting institutions that are not financially independent.
Students and their families will need to be brave. Of course the prospect of debt is worrying but I still see well-dressed students with their new cars, mobile phones and nice flats. Students should accept their responsibilities: they are not going to university to have three or more years of fun. They are going to gain a higher education which should bring them the best jobs in the country. Expecting a contribution to the costs of their education is, therefore, quite reasonable.
Those whose decisions are influenced by the money factor are clearly those who are not committed to what they wish to do. If you want to do something badly enough, you will do it regardless of the costs. In addition,

fees encourage students to select their courses more carefully. Universities will have to look at the future of minority courses and make higher education relate to the demands of the twenty-first century.

Exercise 7 (an example answer)

a) **It is time for one single German education system: one country, one system.**

We managed to unify east and west but why do we ignore north and south – Bavaria and Schleswig-Holstein – or any of the other states, in fact, when it comes to education? Education is for the future benefit of the country – not for Thüringen or Hessen, Sachsen-Anhalt or the Saarland. So isn't it time to have one single system? A single system where everyone knows what is expected. Everyone from parents to employers. A system where standards are equal throughout the country.

Standardisation is an ever more pressing issue. In a society which needs to be more mobile – to go where the jobs are – it's important that obstacles are removed which hinder it. Differences in school systems and their standards are just one such obstacle which could and should be removed.

Standards between states should be the same. An Abitur should not be easier or harder depending upon where one lives. Grades must be comparable. This does not just stop at schools, either. Universities and further educational institutions should also be included.

Keeping many different parallel systems running is inefficient and creates difficulties, too: difficulties for students and children who need to move from one area to another; difficulties for parents who rightly or wrongly may view one school system as easier than another; difficulties for employers who cannot be expected to know the standard of education from one state to the next.

And efficiency? In a time when saving money is such an important governmental concern, isn't it time to save here, too? Save not by reducing funding in schools but save by reducing the bureaucracy and multiplication involved in running sixteen different education authorities when one single one would do.

b) **Let's not have a 'me society'.**

Me? I'm OK.

Poverty. Unemployment. These don't bother me. Who cares about them? I've got money and I'll work for my Dad, anyway.

No money for pensions. That doesn't bother me, I'm still only 17. The most important thing is that my life is OK. That I can go out, have fun – go to discos and parties. I'm not interested in other people's lives, that's their own responsibility.
Is this the society that we want for ourselves? A society where no one is interested in anyone else? Friends, who are not friends? People whose only interest is self-interest? This is not a society, just individuals who happen to live together.
There's nothing wrong with looking after oneself; being concerned about one's own welfare and future, making decisions to benefit one's own life. But people should also consider the world around them, too. Everyone can spare time to help other people so that their lives can be made a little happier, a little easier. People need to know that there are others one can turn to when the going gets tough.
Shouldn't we all be trying in some way to help people in need? Not just the desperately poor in far-away places but also those people who live near us. An old person living alone perhaps, who would welcome someone to talk to for half an hour so the loneliness of a day could be broken. What a different place the world would be if everyone tried to think about other people and not just themselves – to actually care.
Looking after oneself is fine but not at the expense of other people.
'Me? I'm OK. I'm 17, got lots of money and I'll work for my Dad.' What a sorry future, if that's all we have to look forward to. A 'me society', no thanks.

Ihre Meinung ist uns wichtig!

Ihre Anregungen sind uns immer willkommen. Bitte informieren Sie uns mit diesem Schein über Ihre Verbesserungsvorschläge!

Titel-Nr.	Seite	Vorschlag

Bitte hier abtrennen

Zutreffendes bitte ankreuzen!

Die Absenderin/der Absender ist:

- ☐ Lehrer/in in den Klassenstufen: ____
- ☐ Fachbetreuer/in
  Fächer: ____
- ☐ Seminarlehrer/in
  Fächer: ____
- ☐ Regierungsfachberater/in
  Fächer: ____
- ☐ Oberstufenbetreuer/in
- ☐ Schulleiter/in
- ☐ Referendar/in, Termin 2. Staatsexamen: ____
- ☐ Leiter/in Lehrerbibliothek
- ☐ Leiter/in Schülerbibliothek
- ☐ Sekretariat
- ☐ Eltern
- ☐ Schüler/in, Klasse: ____
- ☐ Sonstiges: ____

Unterrichtsfächer: (Bei Lehrkräften!)

____

14-V1M

Bitte ausfüllen und im frankierten Umschlag an uns einsenden. Für Fensterkuverts geeignet.

STARK Verlag
Postfach 1852
85318 Freising

Kennen Sie Ihre Kundennummer? Bitte hier eintragen.

Absender (Bitte in Druckbuchstaben!)

Name/Vorname

Straße/Nr.

PLZ/Ort

Telefon privat

Geburtsjahr

E-Mail-Adresse

Schule/Schulstempel (Bitte immer angeben!)

Bitte hier abtrennen

(Bitte blättern Sie um)

14-V1M

Bestellungen bitte direkt an:
STARK Verlagsgesellschaft mbH & Co. KG · Postfach 1852 · 85318 Freising

STARK